LEVERAGED FINANCE:
How to Raise and Invest Cash

Also by the author—

How to Pyramid Small Business Ventures Into a Personal
  Fortune
Thirty-Six Small Business Mistakes—And How to Avoid Them

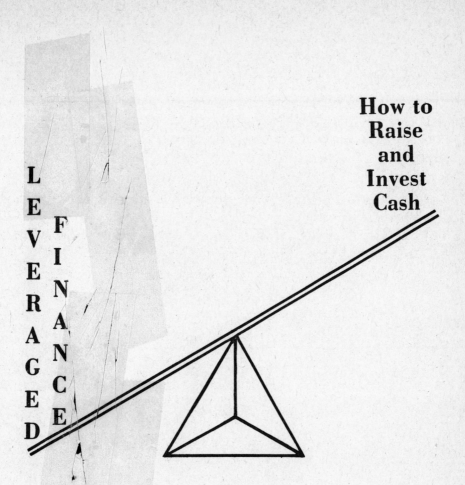

LEVERAGED FINANCE

How to Raise and Invest Cash

by

Mark Stevens

Prentice-Hall, Inc.

Englewood Cliffs, New Jersey

Prentice-Hall, Inc., **London**
Prentice-Hall of Australia, Pty. Ltd., **Sydney**
Prentice-Hall of Canada, Ltd., **Toronto**
Prentice-Hall of India Private Ltd., **New Delhi**
Prentice-Hall of Japan, Inc., **Tokyo**
Whitehall Books, Ltd., Wellington, **New Zealand**

Second Printing . . . . . February, 1981

©1980, by

Mark Stevens

Library of Congress Cataloging in Publication Data

Stevens, Mark
  Leveraged finance.

  Includes index.
  1. Loans. 2. Small business—Finance. I. Title
HG3751.S7   658.1'522   79-23897
ISBN 0-13-535104-9

Printed in the United States of America

To Cheryl, whom I love and am proud of and enjoy—
and whose love has always helped me through.

HOW THIS BOOK
WILL HELP YOU

Capital is the fuel that powers business. Whether the objective is to launch a new venture, bring an invention to market, or expand a going concern, cash is required in substantial amounts. Cash is needed for raw materials, components, trained personnel, stores, plants and advertising. The lack of adequate cash prevents many otherwise excellent projects from getting off the ground.

I don't believe that ever needs to happen. In my position as a nationally syndicated financial columnist—in touch with entrepreneurs, bankers, government officials and industrialists across the nation—I have witnessed case after case of tough, strong-willed business people who have managed to achieve extraordinary success without much money of their own. Their secret: harnessing the compelling financial force of **leveraging**. Put simply, this is a method that lets you use other people's cash to work for you in building a major business enterprise.

Although they have been used by giant corporations for years, the possibilities of **leveraging** have remained relatively unfamiliar to many owners, managers, and financial executives of small and middle sized companies. In this book, the **leveraging** concept is fully explained at last. It's all here in everyday language; in a step-by-step formula (complete with charts, profiles and a **leveraging** glossary) for implementing this powerful technique.

This book does much more than reveal dozens of loan sources and explain dozens of cash-raising techniques. Readers learn where to turn for little-known government loans—from the EPA, LDC's or the SBA—how to get life insurer private placements or growth capital funds. They learn techniques for "going public" without all the red tape the giant corporations need and much, much more. You get more than just ideas in this book, you get names, addresses and executive contacts.

And most importantly, you learn how to use the power of **leveraging**—how to harness it to do what you want—to magnify the value of the money you personally raise many times over. You will read the case histories of people who have parceled out small quantities of cash to numerous **leveraged** ventures, enabling them to control vast business interests with a relatively small pool of funds. One of the nation's leading businessmen, now chairman of a billion-dollar-a-year conglomerate, started this way and continues to use this principle.

There is no magic involved in using **leveraging**. There are no real mysteries. Just an ingenious and proven concept for raising and investing cash in a way that can most effectively nurture thriving business ventures, so lack of cash need no longer hold you back. You'll learn, for example, just how to:

- Compute precisely how much cash you need.
- The ideal sources of cash you should turn to, what they expect from you and how to get the most from them.
- How to design a prime lender profile to get you your money.
- How to use the language of **leveraging** (including a complete glossary of terms) to speak to financiers in their own jargon, since familiarity with their language goes a long way toward winning their confidence.
- How to design a balance sheet that helps raise cash.
- How to use **the elevator principle** to translate your growing business success into personal wealth.

Although names, places, and dollar amounts cited in this book have been changed, all examples cited are based on similar or typical cases observed by or related to the author. The techniques, strategies, suggestions and other information cited in this book are based on the author's professional experience but do not imply any guarantee of commercial or financial success.

Mark Stevens

CONTENTS

LEVERAGED FINANCE:
How to Raise and Invest Cash

YES, CAPITAL
IS AVAILABLE

MONEY: No topic so attracts the interest of established business owners, as well as those first thinking of being their own boss, as the topic of cold, green cash. Everyone knows that money goes to money—getting started in business means coming up with that first investment, and later expansion demands a continued flow of capital.

Capital, after all, is the fuel that powers the engines of business. Every commercial venture, large and small, new and established, requires capital investments to get the wheels spinning, to grow and prosper as a successful enterprise. Capital builds the facilities, purchases the equipment, hires the personnel, sponsors the advertising and provides for the customer services that enable most businesses to function. Capital builds the company from scratch, nurtures it as it finds its niche in the marketplace and then generates the wherewithal for future growth.

This fact of business life has led many otherwise capable entrepreneurs to lay down and play dead. Recognizing that they had little capital of their own, they gave up trying to start or expand a business. Imagine this—a man or woman has an excellent commercial concept, plans a very promising product or service and the managerial skills to make it all work—and they never put their ideas into practice simply because there's not enough money in the till to cover all the start-up or expansion costs.

This kind of situation can only be described as wasteful—wasteful of energy, talent and profit potential. The truth is that any idea that is good enough to make money will be able to find the money required to make it succeed. It may take effort and persistence, yes, but in the long run the cash will be there to get the ball rolling. The fatal mistake is to assume that you, as the business owner, must come up with all of the money yourself. This is a nation that has based its industrial might on credit—the Fortune 500 relies on it and so can you.

The entrepreneurs with real savvy have always recognized that there is no rule stating that you must invest your own money. The art and science of leveraging—that is, building a business on borrowed funds—is the real secret of making it big with little personal risk. And most important, leveraging gives you a foot in the door—a means of achieving business success even when you have little capital of your own to invest.

Take the case of the man now considered to be one of the finest fashion designers in the world, Yves St. Laurent. A child prodigy in the world of fashion, St. Laurent was, at age 16, one of the master designers in the great French couture house of Dior. At 21, St. Laurent was running Dior and was acknowledged as the most powerful influence in the French apparel industry. But still, incredibly, he wanted more: a company in his own name—one in which the profits would be his.

A sharp businessman as well as a talented artist, St. Laurent recognized that the only thing standing in the way of his dream was capital. He needed lots of it for manufacturing, showrooms, staff and publicity. The sum required far exceeded St. Laurent's personal resources. Did this stop the designer from fulfilling his potential, from going ahead with the plan that he knew would be extraordinarily profitable? Absolutely not. In spite of the fact that he encountered some resistance from traditional lending sources, St. Laurent persisted and shortly made contact with a wealthy Georgia businessman who had faith in the young designer and was willing to back his first venture. Later, St. Laurent hooked up with Charles of the Ritz, which bought the rights to his name in the U.S.

A MASTER OF LEVERAGED FINANCE

The essential point is this: By relying mostly on the capital supplied by others, St. Laurent built a world-renowned couture business under his own label and he became the darling of wealthy jet-setters from New York to Rome. Later, he translated this fame and prestige into a major, mass production apparel company, Rive Gauche, with stores and boutiques the world over, including shops in many of the leading department stores like Bloomingdale's and Saks Fifth Avenue. Today, St. Laurent is among the wealthiest men in the world of fashion: His companies generate more than $100 million a year.

Yet, he still knows how to leverage his ventures—how to use other people's money to finance his projects. When the designer launched his $100 per ounce perfume called **Opium**, in the fall of 1978, he held a publicity party for it on a Chinese clipper ship docked at New York's South Street Seaport. The one-night affair—which included disco dancing, unlimited champagne, steak tartare, oysters, an extravagant fireworks display, Chinese sword dancers and a guest list featuring Jackie Onassis, Woody Allen, New York's Mayor Edward Koch and Governor Hugh Carey—garnered widespread press coverage for **Opium** and gave the product a fabulous head start in the marketplace. The tab for the event, however, a grand total of $250,000, was picked up by Charles of the Ritz, **not** St. Laurent.

Surprising as it may seem to the inexperienced, raising cash for business needs can just about always be done if the person's skills or ideas are worthy of capital investments. As someone once said

"There is no such thing as undiscovered genius." Those with that kind of "smarts" manage to make themselves heard, manage to make an impression on the world. The same is true with good business ideas: Be persistent and you will find a capital source willing and able to bring it to life.

Not that getting business financing is always easy, sometimes it is and sometimes it is not. But you aren't expected to rely on luck or on the law of averages. The most important thing about using the power of leveraged finance is knowing where to look for credit and capital. That is exactly what I will show you: how to get the inside track on the most lucrative and consistent loan sources. Furthermore, I will show you how to apply the principle of leveraging to multiply the power of your borrowed funds.

*   *   *   *   *   *

As you start out on the journey of using leveraged finance, discard the common notion that the road to borrowed capital is a sort of single-lane highway. With this kind of thinking, the first roadblock or barrier will lead to defeatist attitudes. Actually, there are hundreds of streets and avenues leading to capital sources. A roadblock on one means you'll just have to detour and try another. Remember, there are dozens of different types of governmental loans (local, state and federal), a wide range of private loans and a myriad of ways of raising capital through other financial devices. Depending on the kind of business you are running or planning, and the element of risk involved, you may start off trying for one type of loan and then gradually work your way through the list until you come up with the needed cash.

When Neal F. of Paterson, New Jersey started his professional consulting business, he turned to an "executive credit" outfit and got the $22,000 he needed in less than three weeks—and he did it all through the mail. As a licensed professional engineer with an excellent track record and relatively small capital requirements, Neal had the good fortune of winning approval from his very first loan source.

"The loan was just what I needed to get started on my own," Neal says. "I set up an office, purchased communications equipment to help me stay in touch with the office while I was out in the field and did some limited promotion work to build up contacts in the engineering business.

"The first month was very slow because it took some time for the contacts I was making to take hold and turn into real business leads. But then, by the middle of the second month, I was getting consulting jobs at the rate of at least one per week. After only six months, I had so much new business that the entire loan was paid off and I was earning a net profit of about $72,000 on an annual basis"

The process wasn't nearly as easy, however, for long-time merchant Harry B. of Yonkers, N.Y. When Harry wanted to close up his BP gasoline service station and get into the fast-growing field of unpainted furniture, he needed $262,000 to build a sizable store and purchase an extensive inventory. Since Harry only had $42,000 of his own money, and because he had no previous experience in furniture retailing, all of the commercial banks gave him thumbs down on his loan applications.

"True, I never sold a stick of furniture in my life before going into the business, but I'd damn near sold everything else." Harry explains. "When you are a merchant, when it's in your blood to sell, there's no one who can tell you that you need special experience to handle a certain line. I'd sold bedding, auto parts, life insurance, clothing and even original oil paintings—so I knew I'd have no trouble selling unpainted furniture."

Harry's self-confidence gave him the gumption to press on after nine banks and two commercial finance outfits turned him down. He knew full well that there is more than one road to willing loan sources and that by using the shotgun approach, the business owner is likely to hit at least one bullseye. It proved true in Harry's case: he finally went straight to a firm of furniture manufacturers and appealed to them for financing.

"I made them an offer they couldn't refuse," Harry quips. "What I did was to use my $42,000 as a down payment on the best piece of commercial real estate in Yonkers. The land suddenly came on the market and I grabbed it up quickly. With deed in hand, I went straight to one of the furniture manufacturers that I knew was trying to break into the big Yonkers market. My deal to them was this: I have the location. You come up with the financing to build my store and the trade credit to start my inventory and I'll agree to feature only your goods. And, as a kicker, I warned them that if they turned me down, I was heading right for the competition with the same offer.''

There was no need for that. Allwood Industries, Harry's suppliers, took him up on the offer and built him a beautiful furniture shop right on the prized real estate off bustling Central Avenue. For an investment of only $42,000 Harry bought himself a store, inventory and advertising worth $352,000—considerably more than his original estimate. More important, the venture prospered from the start, caught the unpainted furniture boom just as it was starting to generate hefty sales, and made more money for Harry than he'd ever earned in his life. Three years later, when Harry was ready to sell out and move up to the bigger leagues by purchasing a three-branch auto dealership, he was able to sell the furniture business for a cool $1.3 million profit.

Harry's case is important for two reasons. First, it is indicative of the fact that there are many loan sources which are rarely, if ever, tapped by the less experienced entrepreneurs. Supplier credit, for example, which accounted for part of the deal Harry worked out, is an obscure, yet excellent form of financing which will be explained, in detail, in later chapters. Put simply, however, this is where your supplier extends merchandise to you under highly-favorable repayment conditions. It is a good example of a free enterprise private loan.

Harry's case is also important because it illustrates the power of positive thinking. Harry simple refused to be denied; he refused to be stopped from what he knew would be a great success. It is equivalent to the now famous case of Sylvester Stallone, writer and star of the box office smash movie **Rocky**. Although he was considered a joke by virtually all of the big Hollywood studios, Stallone hung in there until he found a producer willing to back the movie the way Stallone thought it should be done. He got what he sought and there's no denying who was the big winner. The film went on to become one of the biggest of all time and, a year after it came out, Stallone got his first check for $1 million. Best of all, he never put up a dime to earn it.

Positive thinking forces the business person to track down every possible avenue of financing—to leave no stone unturned. This alone improves the chances for success by 80 percent. More important, however, positive thinking tends to be contagious: your certainty of success is likely to rub off on those in position to lend you the money. Remember, every investor wants a sure thing, but they all know that's one assurance they can never get. So they compromise and set their sights on those opportunities most apt to succeed. Here's where your personal salesmanship comes in. You must sell yourself as well as your business idea. The more confident and positive you appear, the better your chances of getting money.

Use this six-step process to prepare yourself for the capital search:

1. Determine the precise type of business that you want to start or expand and write it down in simple terms. No more than two sentences. Clear concepts are easiest to sell.

2. Make sure that you have figured all the angles and that the business will succeed. Give yourself at least a week to stew on this.

3. Once you have determined that the plan is sound and virtually foolproof, spend some time convincing yourself that you can make it work and that you will make money at it.

4. Bring all the confidence you can muster to the interviews with prospective loan sources. Never reveal any doubts about your abilities or your business plan.

5. Be flexible and cooperative. Make every effort to provide the prospective lender with additional information, if requested. Remember, any defensiveness on your part will be viewed as a sign of weakness.

6. Do not give up. If you are convinced that your brainstorm will work, keep trying until you find someone to lend you the money or extend the needed credit. Tap the various types of loan sources listed in this book.

* * * * * * *

Before we go any further, let's take a closer look at the concept of "leveraged finance." Webster's Seventh New Collegiate Dictionary defines "leverage" as the "action of a lever or the mechanical advantage gained by it." Additionally, the dictionary says that "leverage" is "effectiveness and power."

The last part is crucial—"effectiveness and power." This is precisely what leveraged finance can do for your business. It can magnify its strengths and resources by several times their real value and can enable you to participate in the bigger deals, where the real profits are. The concept of leveraging frightens many entrepreneurs simply because they are not familiar with how it works and because they let the sound of the term scare them away. Actually, the principle of leveraging is used widely in many parts of our daily lives. The difference is that in these circumstances, we don't recognize it for what it is.

Take stock purchases, for example. If you have a margin account and buy securities for less than their current market value, you are using the concept of leveraging to get a bigger piece of the action than you might otherwise afford. You are using other people's money to speculate. Let's say stock in Howard Johnson Co. is selling on the New York Stock Exchange for $10 a share. You want to control 5000 shares of the stock because you believe, from a secret report that you've read, that the stock will soon experience a sharp increase in price. To control that 5000 shares through the traditional approach, you would call your broker, order the shares and send him a check for $50,000. If the stock goes up 10 points, you'll make a tidy $50,000 profit: for every dollar invested, you got $2 back. Not bad.

But it can be better. Perhaps you didn't have the $50,000 to put up in the first place. Or maybe you had $50,000 but could only afford to play with $25,000. Does that mean that you would have to miss out on what you considered to be a sure thing? Or would you be forced to settle for a smaller profit? Absolutely not. Smart money people open a margin account with their broker. This enables the trader to purchase the full 5000 shares while only putting up, say, half the money, or $25,000. This means that you are controlling 5000 shares for the real cost of controlling only 2500 shares.

Here's where the real beauty of this comes in: Let's assume, once again, that the price of Howard Johnson stock does rise 10 points. This time you made that $50,000 profit while putting up only $25,000. You invested $25,000 and got back $100,000. So now, every dollar invested returned $4, not $2. That's the power of leveraging.

The same phenomenon occurs in as simple a transaction as buying a house. It's a perfect example of leveraging, the only difference being you probably never called it that. For example, if you have $30,000 cash on hand, and a pretty good income, you can do two things when it comes to buying a house. First, you can look for a house that costs $30,000, plunk your cash down and live there. Certainly, you will not have a very big nor a very nice house—not with $30,000. Nor will you have the tax benefits of paying off a mortage, in which case Uncle Sam really bears part of the cost of the home.

The second option, and a far wiser one to be sure, is to use that $30,000 as a "lever" to purchase a large, comfortable home in the $100,000 range. Here, you get a superior standard of living, tax deductions from your mortgage interest payments and a personal asset that will most likely appreciate in value significantly over the years. What's more, since you have up to 30 years to pay for the home, you will be paying for much of it with grossly devalued dollars.

Look what leveraging lets you do:

1. For only $30,000 down you enjoy the comfort and luxuries of a $100,000 lifestyle.

2. You get substantial tax benefits which mean, in effect, that the government is sharing in the cost of the home.

3. You get a leveraged or magnified yield on your investment. If you put that $30,000 cash into a $30,000 home, and, assuming a 10 percent annual increase in home values, your first year paper gain on the investment would be $3000. If, on the other hand, you bought the $100,000 house, your $30,000 cash investment would produce a first paper gain of $10,000. That significant difference shows what can be accomplished with wise use of leveraged capital.

So you see that leveraging, in its basic forms, is a fairly common technique. It is simply called by other names such as mortgages and margin accounts. This is important to recognize because it illustrates that we are all somewhat familiar with some types of leveraging strategies. To put the concept to its most potent use, however, you must apply it to business operations. Here's where you can really use it to build a fortune.

* * * * * *

As I have mentioned—and this is contrary to popular opinion—there are scores of lucrative financing sources available to small business. (I will cover these, in full, in later chapters.) Raising your initial capital through one of these sources is, however, only the first step in an integrated program that truly harnesses the power of leveraged finance.

HOW CASH POWER IS MAGNIFIED

My strategy will show you how to parcel out these funds into a series of money-making ventures that may or may not be related. In other words, you can use some of your own funds or fixed assets to raise cash many times the worth of what you have. You then turn around and reinvest this new flow of capital into other leveraged positions. By the time you are fully invested, your original stake may be controlling business interests up to 100 times their worth. This is how a small business owner can get very big, very fast.

That is precisely how a young man, now in his 30s, got to be where he is today; he runs one of the nation's largest financial services companies. His name is Saul Steinberg and the company he runs called Reliance Group boasts more than 8000 employees and more than $1 billion per year in revenues. Better than almost anyone else in this country, Steinberg understands the power of leveraged finance and his great success is testimony to what it can do for one person's fortune and for their business interests.

To make a long story short, Steinberg graduated from Wharton Business School with the seemingly foolhardy intention of competing with IBM. He believed that he could lease used computers to companies that did not require the latest generation of computer hardware. Borrowing $100,000 on the strength of his idea, he started his company and called it Leasco.

This was in the early 1960s—a so-called "go-go" period in the stock market when hot new ideas got rapid financing. Steinberg's company caught the attention of the "street" which started to believe that the young man might have a good idea after all. After some signs of early success, Steinberg used these encouraging prospects as selling points to take his company public. He sold shares of stock in Leasco, thereby raising millions of dollars in additional capital. Now the fledgling firm had the fuel to test its founder's ideas to the fullest potential.

Again, the early going was encouraging, Leasco became the darling of the public and of Wall Street analysts, and soon the price of the stock was soaring to many times its original value: at one point the shares climbed well over $100 each. This price was based on speculation: it was many times the company's actual earnings. The important point, however, is that Steinberg set out to use the jacked-up value of his stock as a lever to pry his way into even bigger business interests. By offering to exchange shares of Leasco for shares of huge companies whose stocks were then undervalued, Steinberg could wrest control of these giants.

He started at the top. Steinberg's first takeover target was one of the nation's largest and oldest banks. The only thing that stopped him from succeeding was a special session of the New York State legislature, called specifically to thwart the young entrepreneur. Later, Steinberg turned his attention to Reliance Insurance Co., an old line Philadelphia-based outfit then doing more than half a billion dollars a year in sales. This time, he pulled off the takeover and found himself, at age 29, at the helm of a financial giant. Before he was 30, Steinberg was worth more than $50 million—almost all of it on his ability to leverage that original $100,000 stake into greater and greater amounts. Today he lives in a huge Manhattan townhouse—the former residence of the Rockefeller family.

Certainly, not every leveraging strategy will achieve these lofty heights, but that is not the important point. What is important is that you are learning the great power of leveraging—it can be used to borrow money and to magnify limited resources to many times their actual worth. And you are learning that you can use other people's money to launch or to expand your business. There is really no limit to how high you can climb if you recognize this power, learn to master it and have confidence in your own abilities.

CHECKING YOURSELF

Before you go any further, however, take a closer look at yourself. Building a successful business through the power of leveraging is not as easy as baking a cake. You are smart enough to know that nothing good in life is that easy. A fair amount of intelligence, persistence, hard work and business aptitude are required to make a real go of your leveraging strategies. The first step, then, is to see if you are up to the challenge.

You have probably never tried to measure or analyze your personality traits before, so this may be a novel procedure for you. If so, don't shy away from it or get nervous that you'll fail. There is no pass or fail grade here, but instead, an indication of whether or not you are the kind of person likely to make maximum use of the leveraged finance concept. For those of you first starting out in business, the personality analysis can reveal whether or not you are cut out to run a business; for established entrepreneurs, the analysis can tell if you are up to the challenge of building a much larger organization.

Take the personality profile on page 27, recording your scores on a separate piece of paper.

Consider any score of 75 or better to be indicative of a clear aptitude to perform well as a leveraged financier. Although lower scores certainly do not mean immediate disqualification, the closer you are to 75 or beyond the more your natural abilities are matched for the challenges ahead. Those with scores of 100 or more are supremely qualified.

Let's look at this another way: What are the things that cause most business owners to fail? Dun & Bradstreet Inc., the national credit and financial services outfit, found, in one of its comprehensive studies, the following revealing data:

1. Among retail merchants, those selling apparel are generally among the groups suffering the highest failure rates.

2. The vast majority of commercial failures in all business categories are due to liabilities of from $5000 to $100,000. Negligible financial difficulties—amounts of less than $5000—account for less than four percent of the total failures.

3. The greatest number of failures, 42.7 percent, were due to liabilities of from $25,000 to $100,000. The remaining failure distribution, by liability, was as follows: 27.2 percent, $5000 to $25,000; 23.5 percent, $100,000 to $1 million; and 2.8 percent more than $1 million.

	LIMITED	AVERAGE	SUPERIOR
I have previous business experience	5	10	15
I have direct selling experience	5	10	15
I have a good mind for mathematics	5	10	15
I have had training or experience in business accounting and finance.	5	10	15
I have used borrowed capital and/or credit lines for business start-up or expansion.	5	10	15
I am ambitious and hard driving	5	10	15
I am always looking for new challenges	5	10	15
I have leadership qualities	5	10	15
I inspire confidence in friends, family, employees	5	10	15
I have confidence in myself	5	10	15

4. Sixty percent of all retail business failures occur within the first five years of operation. Although the first year appears to be the safest (only two percent of retail failures occur during this period), this seems to be the result of "holding actions" rather than early fiscal health. In fact, the initial 12 months of a new business venture is often the incubation period for developing problems.

5. The problems that remain below the surface during the first year often gather destructive force during the following years. The percentage rates for retail failures, for example, during the following three-year period are 16, second year; 19.1, third year; and 14.6, fourth year. The statistics for other business categories—wholesale, manufacturing, construction and services—are similar.

This age-failure distribution has changed little over the past 25 years, indicating the same mistakes that plagued small business operations a quarter century ago are still being made. The high failure rate in the early years supports the widespread belief that many individuals start business ventures without sufficient preparation. In most instances, they lack the necessary capital and experience, and fail to devote substantial time to long-range planning. Managerial deficiencies account for up to 93 percent of all failures.

So here is carefully researched evidence of the need to master the techniques of leveraged finance. Drawing together the essentials of the Dun & Bradstreet study, it is evident that most companies fail to survive and grow because they run into financial difficulties that management is incapable of surmounting, and it's not the small amounts that take the greatest toll. No. About 70 percent are due to liabilities of from $25,000 to $1 million. Just about anyone can raise $5000 or less. That is not the challenge. It is the big sums that are harder to come by and that can deprive otherwise sound ventures of their maximum potential.

It is this very process of raising money and magnifying its value into huge sums that leveraged finance is all about. This is what you will learn to do.

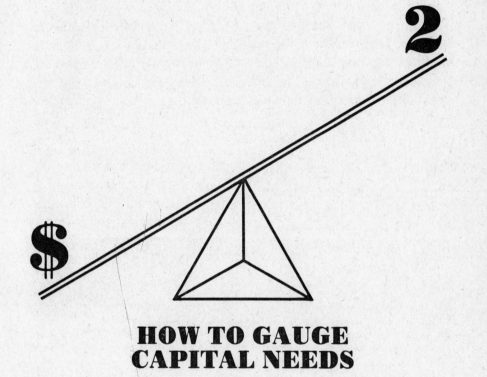

HOW TO GAUGE
CAPITAL NEEDS

Let us repeat the one lesson that must remain indelibly etched in your mind as you start or expand a business: Poor management, especially as it relates to financial know-how, is responsible for the vast majority of business failures. And it is the big amounts of money, not the petty figures, that wind up sinking firms. Most dead ventures go under because management is not well versed in the powers of leveraged finance. The owners are helpless to revive the firms because most believe that this must be done with their own financial resources. You are learning a better way.

ESTIMATING NEEDS

Still, regardless of how a business owner handles his finances, one factor is a universal prerequisite to good management: that is, planning, as accurately as possible, just how much money the business will need to get started, to expand and to meet its growth objectives.

This is never an easy task. The very thinking that this is something that can be done by instinct or by seat-of-the-pants action is precisely what gets many business owners into trouble. They simply do not take this part of the planning process seriously enough and more often than not wind up underestimating the amount of capital required.

It is wise to think of the capital planning process as if you are the skipper of a superb sailing craft equipped with auxiliary engines. Let's say you are about to embark on a long sea voyage and that you must reach your destination on a given date. How much fuel would you take for the auxiliary engines? True, the vessel will go most of the way under the power of the winds. But conditions may require that, from time to time, you switch to engine power.

Determining precisely how much fuel you will need demands extensive research and mathematical computations. How long is the voyage in terms of actual distance? What are projected weather conditions on the route? How much time do you have to get to the destination? What is the vessel's sailing speed? What is its rate of fuel consumption? Keeping in mind that the ship will likely go most of the way under its own power, you still must have sufficient fuel aboard to get it from point C to point D at times when sailing is impossible. In conducting your research and computations you may stick to the averages: average winds of the sea route, average weather conditions, average speed of the boat and so forth. The problem is—and every good skipper as well as business manager knows this—the averages don't always hold true. Your voyage may be that one in a thousand where winds are almost nonexistent. You'll need much more fuel than planning strictly by the averages would have called for.

The same is true in planning your capital requirements for business. Basing your assumptions on optimum or average conditions can mean you'll wind up in mid-stream without enough steam to accomplish your objectives. You simply cannot assume that your sales will match the industry average, that revenues will grow in orderly progression month by month and that you will not encounter serious setbacks in the early going. You may, unfortunately, have a hard time getting established, making a name for your firm or getting adequate supplies from your distributors. And although you may wind up being extremely successful in the long run, you'll be able to hang in there for that taste of success only if you have enough of a bankroll to get you through the unexpected problems. So the bottom line is this: When planning capital requirements, be super-cautious and conservative. Anticipate the worst. It's always better to raise more than you need rather than less.

HOW A SUCCESSFUL BUSINESS WAS DEVELOPED

What can happen to buffet a fledgling business is illustrated by the early experiences of Halston, one of our nation's wealthiest and most powerful apparel designers. As an up and coming hat designer for Bonwit Teller stores in the beginning of the 1960's Halston started making a name for himself in New York's fashion circles. As a result, he was graduating from hats to dresses and complete outfits for a few very chic and wealthy clients. Still, this was all on a small, although prestigious, scale.

Halston's budding reputation, however, caught the attention of top executives at Bloomingdale's Department Store, which was then emerging as the world's premier emporium for trendy apparel. Bloomingdale's president at the time, Harold Krensky (now president of the parent firm Federated Department Stores), liked Halston's work and believed the young man had great potential. As a result, Bloomingdale's offered Halston more than he could have ever dreamed of: his own private boutique in the main Bloomingdale's store in Manhattan. It was the designer's chance to really break out on his own—to develop a major business and a national reputation to match.

The deal was that Halston had to go out, raise capital, produce a clothing line, and ready it for sale at the boutique. Since Bloomingdale's is a high volume department store for expensive fashion (it's sales of $400 per square foot are the highest in the industry), Halston had to come up with significant amounts of capital to produce adequate inventories. Stores like Bloomingdale's demand a lot from their suppliers.

Here's where Halston showed his business acumen as well as his artistic abilities. Knowing that he was still a minor force in the fashion business—and that he was relatively powerless to have things his way—Halston raised more money than it seemed that he would really need to get his new company started. This proved to be a smart move indeed.

Halston designed a line of art deco-inspired sweaters and accessories and contracted with an apparel manufacturer to produce the clothing. This is common practice; very few of the big-name designers actually make their own goods. Still, the established names have clout with the manufacturers. Since they can assure the manufacturers of substantial business, they get excellent service and good quality control.

Halston, at this point, had no such power—as he was soon to discover. At the very last minute, his contractor backed out of the deal, leaving Halston with no one to produce his line for the Bloomingdale's boutique. The chance in a lifetime for an emerging designer would be lost if he could not come up with a substitute manufacturer. This delay, however, would cost money. Fabrics which were already purchased and delivered would have to be rerouted; interest expenses on financed materials would mount; and there were substantial expenses involved in tracking down a new contractor.

"This is a business that is based on raw power," Halston explains. "People will make commitments to you but will think nothing of breaking them if a better deal comes along. That's what happened to me in those days when I was first getting started. The contractor just had an opportunity to make more money serving someone else, so he backed out on our deal. I was left holding the bag. I had to continue to support a business that was bringing in no money—certainly we couldn't bring in money until we produced the goods and delivered them to Bloomingdale's."

Fortunately, Halston had the leveraged funds required to keep the firm floating until another production deal could be signed, and sometime later another deal was indeed made. The merchandise was ready and delivered at the 11th hour, the boutique glowed with the new designer's collection and Halston was on his way to the top. The rest, as they say, is history: Halston's enterprises, now a division of the huge conglomerate Norton Simon Inc., rake in over $120 million a year. Halston is into everything from linens to mink coats, he's an international celebrity and his lifestyle is self-described as "opulent."

But, just remember this: Without sufficient funds to get over the initial hurdles, without being able to deliver for Bloomingdale's, Halston may have been written off as a loser—may have lost his only big chance for great success. So we see the importance of carefully planning capital requirements.

*   *   *   *   *   *

To a great extent, the amount of money required to start or expand a business is determined by the company's field or industry. Some types of business are labor intensive, others require sophisticated technology and some are capital intensive. It is the latter category which demands the greatest amounts of cash and/or credit. Generally speaking, heavy manufacturing and those businesses requiring very costly inventories (like diamonds and fine art) are the most capital intensive; service firms, on the other hand, usually need the least amount of start-up or expansion capital.

Some businesses are so capital intensive that small business people are advised to stay away. There's no sense fooling yourself—or wasting your time, talents and finances—on a venture that just demands more than an individual entrepreneur can come up with. Yes, leveraged finance can magnify the power of your cash resources many times over, but not enough to put you into some of the really heavy, capital-intensive industries. Count among these utilities, airlines, mainframe computers and automobiles.

The last is a good example because it represents the kind of so-called glamor industry many entrepreneurs have, at one time or another, had dreams of getting involved in. The American love affair with the automobile is famous: Many of us have entertained visions of designing that one super sports car, right out of a James Bond film, that everyone would want to buy.

This dream has led modern enterpreneurs to try to enter the auto manufacturing business, but with very few positive results. The capital requirement for even the simplest production facilities (one model/one style) can easily reach $1 billion including promotion and sales costs. And that's just the tip of the iceberg. Model changes and the introduction of new models to expand the initial line can run well into many billions of dollars.

Even established, proven and highly-regarded automobile executives have a very difficult time raising sufficient capital to go it on their own as auto makers. Perhaps the best recent example is that of John Z. De Lorean, once a golden boy vice-president of General Motors, responsible for the company's North American operations. Promoted to this position while still in his forties, and earning about $500,000 a year at it, DeLorean was considered by many to be in line for the top GM spot.

Then he abruptly quit. A man with a penchant for an exciting lifestyle and for beautiful women, DeLorean did not feel comfortable with the staid and conservative atmosphere at GM's Detroit headquarters. Seeking the thrill and the excitement of running his own show, DeLorean gave up the GM vice presidency to launch his own car company.

The going has not been easy. In spite of DeLorean's prestigious image in the auto industry, and in spite of the fact that he was well known to investors throughout the international business community, DeLorean had difficulty raising money and getting his venture on stream. As of the writing of this book, plans to build the first DeLorean factory were changed at the last minute from a location in Puerto Rico to one in Ireland (both governments offer exceptional tax advantages to companies locating there). In addition, DeLorean was still short of his ideal capital resources and production had not yet begun. Once the wheels of production start moving, any pre-existing capital shortages tend to become exaggerated by cost overruns. Although DeLorean may, in fact, prove to be profitable, I recommend that individual entrepreneurs stay away from such extraordinarily capital-intensive businesses like auto manufacturing. Consider anything in the $1 billion category to be over your head unless and until your leverage strategy puts you, like it did for Saul Steinberg, in a position to capitalize on highly-magnified personal or corporate wealth. Once you achieve this status, there's no limit to how high you can shoot. Although his case is certainly the exception rather than the rule, we noted how Steinberg was able to shoot high enough to come within inches of taking over a giant bank—and he did succeed in acquiring a huge insurance company.

*   *   *   *   *   *

CAPITAL NEEDS OF TRADITIONAL BUSINESSES

How much capital will you need for the more traditional businesses, ones more suitable for independent entrepreneurs? Take a look at retailing, for example. Opening a shop or expanding a chain of stores is a popular move with independent business owners. Many of the great personal fortunes have been and still are being made by those with the foresight and ability to sell merchandise on a limited basis and then to graduate to the bigger leagues. In fact, many established business owners with one or two stores already generating healthy profits, often look for new and unrelated opportunities in which to reinvest. This is often a mistake. The effort should be made, through leveraging, to stay in the business the entrepreneur knows best—but to expand it dramatically. Why invest in a strange and unfamiliar business when the one or two stores already owned could be parlayed into 10, 30, or 100? By staying in the business that you know best and in which you have a proven track record, you decrease your risks and improve your chances of securing growth capital and credit. Investors are more apt to back you if you can prove expertise in the business.

What does it cost to build a modern retail store? Well, let's look at this from two perspectives: a modest-sized store or local chain or a big regional or national operation. The costs vary greatly depending on the scale you are operating on.

If you are building a store from scratch, land prices differ widely across the country, ranging anywhere from $10,000 to $200,000 per acre for commercial real estate. For our purposes, let's figure $50,000 an acre and that we will need three acres for the building plus parking. Actual construction costs, including interior work, run about $50 per square foot. This can easily zoom up to $80-90 a square foot if elaborate interiors (cathedral ceilings, sunken rooms, heavy use of glass) are planned.

Next question: How big a store will you need? Here again, needs vary greatly according to the type of business. Obviously, companies with big-ticket items like pianos, televisions and furniture need considerable showroom and warehouse space; apparel shops, jewelry stores and the like need much less room. Let's compromise and say you need a modest store, including office and backroom space, of 3000 square feet.

Although you are planning a small business to be sure, a look at our figures so far indicates that a substantial amount of start-up capital is required. Land and construction costs (based on $50 per square foot) come in at $300,000.

For this considerable sum, all you get is a shell of a building. Before you can actually cut the ribbon and get the register ringing, you'll have to add on these additional costs:

- Interior decorating of the store, including floor and wall coverings, paint, displays and fixtures: $60,000

- Inventory: $50,000

- Insurance: $5000

- Legal and accounting fees: $3000

- Supplies: $3000

- Advertising and Promotion: $10,000

Sub Grand Start-Up Total: $431,000

Add to this the following expenses the business is likely to incur before revenues are great enough to cover the costs:

- Utilities: $3000
- Payroll (including mandatory fringes): $100,000
- General Expenses: $15,000

Grand Start-Up Total: $549,000

Incredible as it may seem, the figures don't lie: considering to-days inflated costs for everything from construction to utilities, it can cost more than half a million dollars to start a modest retail store and to keep it funded during the first year or so of operations. This is based on the assumption that the business will not be profitable—and will be able to cover only a small percentage of its costs—for a full year. Some businesses require less time to come out of the red and stand on their feet; others need considerably more time.

The important point to remember is that the start-up expenses— the amount of capital you must raise—exceeds that wich covers construction, inventory and related costs alone. You must have reserve cash to pay the salaries, the fuel bills and the taxes while the company is still in the developing stages and too weak to pay its own freight.

For established retailers, say the owners of small department stores, major expansion of their businesses can be far more costly. Current thinking holds that for retail organizations to commit to significant geographic expansion, the firms must abide by the so-called "cluster concept."

This holds that for major geographic expansion to be economically sound, the merchant must open not one but between three to five new stores, simultaneously, in a given region. The purpose for this is to achieve economies of scale. The stores can be served by a single, central warehouse; distribution can feed a number of outlets in close proximity to one another; and costs for local advertising can be shared by the company's stores in the area. An ad in the local newpaper, for example, will benefit four or five stores rather than just one.

"After nine years of running a successful children's clothing business on Long Island, New York, I looked up one day and recognized that I was stagnating," says Harlan R. of Plandome, N.Y. "I was doing well, yes, and making a very comfortable living, but I had never used my skills and talents to expand and build a really big business. I simply never pursued the idea and anyway, I had it in the back of my mind that full-scale expansion would require much more capital than I could raise.

"My attitude changed completely, however, after what I initially thought was a purely social visit to my brother's new home outside Boston near Chestnut Hill, Mass. Al had just been relocated there by his employer and my wife Anne and I drove up to visit him. I'd never been to that part of the country before and the trip turned out to be very pivotal in my life. Al impressed me with his almost fanatical belief in the growth prospects for the Boston suburbs and so I drove around with him and checked it out myself. I continued my research upon my return to New York, getting facts and figures from the Chamber of Commerce and a private consulting outfit. It did, indeed, seem like an ideal place to expand my retail business. For the first time in years, I felt really excited about business again—my blood was rushing."

Harlan learned quickly, however, that to expand efficiently to such a distant market, it would be best to build three stores positioned to ring downtown Boston from its outlying suburbs. In addition, he would have to build a substantial-sized central warehouse. Total tab: $2 million including the stores.

"I only had $112,000 in cash of my own, but, to my surprise, that was all I needed to get the project moving," Harlan adds. "The power of leveraging filled in for what I didn't have. My brother came up with some cash and the Long Island banks were willing to foot the rest of the bill with a substantial business loan based on my business history and fixed assets."

Harlan's leverage-based expansion has worked out extremely well. Once the entrepreneur gained confidence and momentum, he took his company, KidsWear, public, raised an additional $13 million in the public markets (the technique of "going public" is discussed in full in Chapter 5) and opened 20 more stores in four states: Connecticut, Pennsylvania, Virginia and Maryland.

*   *   *   *   *   *

USING A FINANCIAL NEEDS CHART

Again, back to the question of how much capital is required to start a business. Since we have said that this varies greatly with the type of business, its size and its location, we can only provide rough guidelines for some of the most common types of business ventures. Use the following chart to estimate your capital requirements*:

automobile service station (purchase of existing unit)	$30,000 to $200,000 depending on location
automobile dealership	$1 to $3 million
light manufacturing business (crafts, garments, novelties)	$500,000 to $1 million
heavy manufacturing business (machinery, vehicles, appliances)	$10 million to $1 billion
liquor store	$500,000
professional practice	$10,000 to $800,000 depending on need for costly equipment
small consulting firm	$15,000 to $250,000 depending on use of staff and computer facilities
manufacturer's representative	$5000 to $100,000

Most figures are based on the assumption that the business will build and own its facilities rather than lease (except for service firms, which need little more than a rented office.) Bear in mind that this chart is meant to be nothing more than a starting point for your capital computations. Once you identify the right field of business and have some idea of the capital requirements, you should begin perfecting your estimate—tailoring it to your specific needs and objectives. Entrepreneurs can come up with a highly-accurate projection of these requirements by taking the following steps:

1. Prepare a written fact sheet describing your proposed business concept or expansion plans in detail. Include the size and number of facilities, staff size for the first two years and other likely expenses.

2. Isolate three prospective business sites and determine the exact costs to rent or build at each.

3. Project your first two years' business sales on a month-by-month basis. Also, prepare a formal cash flow analysis for this period.

4. Contact the trade organization in your present or prospective field and indicate that you would like to become a member. The better trade groups will then help you get started by offering literature, and in some cases trained consultants, which can provide detailed data on current start-up costs. Some of the best information is, in fact, available from the national trade groups. Many keep current average start-up costs, as well as other operating statistics, for companies just like yours throughout the nation. This can be of immense aid in refining your capital requirement estimate.

5. Visit your banker and other prospective loan sources. Be sure to bring along the business fact sheet and financial projections you prepared. Prospective lenders will scrutinize your computations and will use their expertise to determine if, in fact, you have done a good job of estimating your capital needs and income flow. They will make suggestions and changes free of charge—a service that could cost several thousand dollars if you went through private consultants. The lender will further refine your capital estimate. Keep in mind that his projection will most likely be a sound one. The lender will, after all, base his loan decision on it , because he'll be putting up the money and assuming the risk.

6. Make contact with a friend or associate in the same or similar business as yourself. Have this person review your projections. In many

cases, there are hidden costs and opportunities in business operations that only another owner-manager would know about. There is no substitute for practical, hands-on experience.

7. Finally, if you would like another source of information before proceeding with your leverage strategy, you can touch bases with a business consultant. It is important, however, to proceed cautiously here. Many incompetent individuals call themselves business consultants. Since there is no law against this, and no licensing requirements in most cases, they do not have to have any real skills or experience.

We suggest, therefore, that you work only with those consultants who belong to the Institute of Management Consultants. Members of this organization will confer with you about the nature of your venture before accepting the assignment, will agree to fees or the fee basis in advance and will keep your conversations confidential. For further information, including help in selecting a business consultant, contact the Institute of Management Consultants, 347 Madison Ave., New York, N.Y. 10016 212-687-2502.

Free consulting is also available from the Small Business Aministration's field offices and from its related SCORE (Service Corps of Retired Executives) chapters. For the nearest location, check the white pages of your phone book or write the Small Business Administration, 1441 L. St., Washington, D.C. You can also call for free SBA financial publications through this toll-free number 800-433-7212.

A word of caution is in order here: do not be lulled into a false sense of security when dealing with consultants who operate under the auspices of the federal government. Just like private practitioners, their competence varies markedly: some are excellent and some are very poor. Try to get a recommendation from a friend or business associate before trusting yourself to any consultant.

*   *   *   *   *   *

MARKETING NEW IDEAS

When it comes to projecting capital requirements, one type of venture stands apart from all the rest. That is, the marketing of new inventions. This can be the most difficult but also the most rewarding project to tackle.

It is difficult because most investors tend to shy away from new inventions. There's no proof it will actually work or sell—no established track record you can point to. This is the traditional thinking about inventions, but it fails to take into account one powerful factor: imagination. The very fact that new inventions have no track record can be turned around into a positive force. The possibilities for the resulting product are virtually unlimited. Your invention could turn out to be that one in a million jackpot—the hoola hoop, the instant camera or the calculator of tomorrow.

This is the kind of prospect that excites and motivates the more gutsy investors. Sell them the project on these terms and you may get the full financing for the venture before there is even a prototype to show.

To compute how much money you will need to take the invention from drawing board to marketplace, go through the procedures outlined in this chapter, but also make some contact with manufacturing pros and technical experts. You should also be aware that some outfits specialize in bringing new inventions to market. Write or call Pixonic Corp., 22 Walter St., Pearl River, N.Y. 914-735-7774.

"I came up with an invention that would automatically turn the pages of a book or document for a typist, at a rate based on the typist's speed," says Janet L. of Nutley, N.J. "But when I tried to sell the idea to investors, they balked. They didn't know if the product could really be produced and what's more, they shied away from dealing with a woman. They had no confidence in me."

A very smart and crafty entrepreneur in her own right, however, Janet recognized that she would have to sell the idea on its money-making opportunities rather than its technical specifications.

"I knew that if I did my homework and put the invention in a very exciting and promising context, certain types of investors couldn't resist it. And that's just what I did. I contacted a major secretarial school and found out how many professional typists there were in the U.S. With this figure and my projected selling price, I came up with potential sales of $200 million."

That certainly shook the trees. Janet put together a group of investors, including a noted plastic surgeon, who were willing to put up the $1.7 million seed money. Her contribution: Just the idea alone and the knowledge that leveraged finance can help to raise substantial sums.

*   *   *   *   *   *

What percentage of your capital requirements can you expect to raise through leveraging. That depends on your business experience, former success record, the soundness of your new project and the ability to sell yourself. The range is anywhere from 50 percent to 100 percent of the total financing costs (some may be in credit, some in cash).

The best strategy is to prepare the charts and fact sheets discussed in this book and approach each of the capital and credit sources listed in the following chapters (those relevant to your type of business). Remember, in many cases there is no limit to the number of financial sources you can tap. The more you get to back you on favorable terms, the less assets of your own that you have to risk.

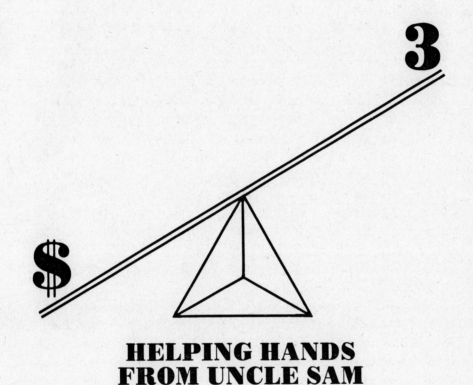

HELPING HANDS
FROM UNCLE SAM

Let's get down to the heart of the matter: All of the principles of leveraged finance come to naught unless you know where to turn for loans, financing and credit. You must know exactly how to locate the money sources necessary to launch the business enterprise and to keep it functioning throughout the growth stages. How to approach and to work with these lenders will be explored in later chapters. For now, our emphasis is on ferreting out the obscure, as well as the well-known, loan sources.

The distinction between the obvious and the obscure is important, because when the inexperienced or untutored entrepreneurs seek out business financing, they tend to concentrate solely on the obvious sources. As a result, all wind up competing for the limited amount of funds available from the most sought after lenders. This is especially true when it comes to direct government and government sponsored loans. Ask any ten business owners what assistance is available in this area and nine will likely refer you to the Small Business Administration (SBA).

What's wrong with that? Only that while the SBA is indeed a prominent source for small business funding (this, in fact, is the SBA's major function), it is also the one government agency beseiged by hundreds of thousands of entrepreneurs for loans. With the relatively small financial resources at its disposal, the SBA must say no to many more loan applications than it approves; and it must reduce the amounts requested on those that do get thumbs up.

Equally important, while concentrating solely on the SBA as a source for government small business funds, owners and those just getting started in business overlook the fact that there are additional sources of government funds completely unrelated to the SBA. By learning about these sources, you will have a leg up on your competitors as well as on other would-be entrepreneurs who are all climbing over one another to get at the SBA. Think of it as being similar to a hundred tourists visiting a strange city and waiting in line for hours to eat in a restaurant that a popular guide book recommends. Since all the tourists tend to read the same travel guide, and never think to ask the natives of the city where to eat, they never find out that across the street from the jammed tourist trap is a gem of a restaurant serving better food at half the price.

SBA loans can be crucial to an integrated program of leveraged finance, to be sure, but the important point to remember is that they are not the only form of government-related loans.

The U.S. government is the richest organization in the world—it has more and spends more than anyone or anything else. We'll show you how to get a piece of the action, from the SBA and from other agencies.

Keep in mind that some of the federal loan programs are available through government agencies, departments, foundations and bureaus that may seem, at first consideration, to have nothing to do with small business funding. And it is true enough that this is only a minor aspect of their operations. But, tucked deep inside a number of huge or obscure governmental offices, there are funding offices— and we have isolated a number of them for you.

The following are among the best sources for government or government-related loans:

•**National Science Foundation Loans:** Remember the old enlistment signs that read "Uncle Sam Wants you". Well, they are up again, only this time for a different purpose. The war against national problems is on and small business owners and managers are needed at the front.

The war is a battle of minds. It pits the nation's best brains against our most pressing problems: environmental pollution, resource depletion and the continuing crisis of the energy shortage. The ammunition is facts, figures and experimentation—the essentials of scientific research.

A MAJOR FOUNDATION'S INTEREST

Sponsoring one attack is the National Science Foundation (NSF)—a very prestigious organization and a major supporter of basic research in the U.S. Armed with an annual budget of close to $1 billion, the National Science Foundation provides corporations, universities and other institutions with grants to conduct original research. The idea is to pave the way for scientific progress and to help the nation face its most serious challenges. To achieve these objectives, there is no more potent combination than money and brain power.

Of special interest to the small business community is the National Science Foundation's Research Applied to National Needs (RANN) program. More specialized than other NSF projects, RANN limits its funding to research directed at solving the nation's existing problems. Grants are awarded to individuals and companies specializing in conservation, pollution control, earthquake detection and the like.

Since it is aware of the inventive spirit of the nation's entrepreneurs, NSF is now encouraging small companies to participate in the RANN program. By doing so, officials hope to build bridges between small business and the scientific community. The goal is to enlist the commercial sector to participate in a national program of applied research.

"We believe that small, inventive companies can play a vital role in improving the quality of life in America," says an official of the NSF who is responsible for small business projects. "Some of our best minds are active in these types of firms and we want to utilize their skills for the common good. That's why we are willing to provide substantial sums of money to small companies capable of conducting applied research."

RANN participation is a real boon to technically-oriented small companies or independent professionals. The grants—which have averaged $120,000 each—enable entrepreneurs to explore a wide range of new horizons without having to beg or borrow adequate funds. Cash for the kinds of high-risk, experimental ventures RANN is willing to finance is very difficult to come by from traditional sources.

"We see to it that small companies have every opportunity to obtain research grants," the NSF official adds. "Besides contacts with our own staff, we also put entrepreneurs in touch with research and development experts at other government agencies. These officials may be willing to fund projects we are not currently considering."

To apply for a RANN grant, owner-managers should take the following steps:

- Submit your idea to RANN officials.
- Officials will discourage the idea if they are not encouraged by it or, if the outlook is more favorable, they will request more information in the form of preliminary proposals.
- The entrepreneur goes ahead and prepares the preliminary proposal, which is a capsulized summary of what your project or venture will entail. This should include data on research objectives, how the final product or technology will be utilized, the anticipated benefits and the estimated costs.
- If the idea is still attractive to NSF officials, they will ask that the grant applicant prepare a formal proposal, which is a more detailed version of the preliminary plan.

About half of the ideas that make it to the formal proposal stage wind up being funded—and that's a pretty good batting average considering the amounts of money involved and the high-risk nature of the projects. Successful applicants get outright grants or contracts, depending on the kind of research involved. In most cases, they can also count on obtaining the rights to commercial applications, although the sponsoring agency must consent.

This last clause—that is, the ability to get the rights on commercial applications—can be the key to the mint for talented entrepreneurs. You'll be developing products and ideas with someone else's money and if you should come up with the next Xerox or Polaroid, you'll get the lion's share of the fortune it will produce. That's leveraged finance in its purest form.

More information on RANN grants and programs is available by writing the National Science Foundation, 1800 G Street N.W., Washington, D.C. 20550.

*   *   *   *   *   *

OBTAINING FUNDS FROM LDC

•Local Development Corporations. Believe it or not, you may find a good source of business financing right in your own backyard (so to speak). A little-known network of lending agencies makes millions of dollars of commercial funds available at the local level.

Known as Local Development Corporations (LDC), the agencies are private corporations sponsored by the Small Business Administration (SBA). LDCs promote small business growth and development in towns and communities across the U.S. by providing the funds to build or renovate factories, stores and warehouses and to purchase capital equipment. Companies unable to finance these assets on their own are often able to lease them from the LDC over a period of years.

"LDCs serve as a sort of bridge between small companies and capital sources," says a top SBA official. "Since the funds are loaned to the LDCs and not to the individual companies, many high-risk outfits which would have difficulty obtaining financing through traditional outlets may be successful through this route.''

LDCs are composed of local residents brought together through incorporation for the purpose of promoting business development. At least 25 members or stockholders are required to start an LDC—and at least 70 percent of this group must live or work in the area to be served by the corporation.

LDCs function as follows: When a small company in the area wants to build a new factory, store or office but does not have sufficient capital of its own, the LDC may borrow funds for the construction from the SBA and/or the banks. The facility is then built for the small business and is leased to it for a period of up to 25 years. At the end of the lease period, the lessor may usually buy the building at a previously-established price.

LDCs finance the building with some of their own capital, by direct SBA loans or through a combination of direct loans and SBA-guaranteed bank loans. The small company's payments to the LDC over the course of the lease cover the principal and interest for the loans. Since most LDCs are nonprofit agencies, payments are kept to the minimum.

By enabling small firms to spread out lease payments over many years, LDCs often provide companies with facilities and equipment they could not otherwise afford. What's more, the amounts involved can be substantial: LDCs can borrow up to $500,000 per company from the SBA.

Although LDCs can not provide funds for working capital, owner-managers can get around this by seeking LDC funds for facilities and standard SBA loans for other business needs. Through this double-financing method, small companies can obtain the equivalent of up to $1 million—all of it at modest interest rates.

The criteria for landing LDC loans is similar to that for obtaining other SBA financing. Companies must demonstrate the likelihood of sustained operations and must show an ability to meet the full terms of the lease. In addition, all building plans must win the approval of local zoning laws and other regulations.

One of the best examples of how LDCs can function is the work going on for the past few years in a formerly-blighted section of Baltimore. Thanks, in part, to the work of LDCs in the area, a run-down area has been rejuvenated and turned into a successful shopping center. LDCs have made more than 20 loans there and one of the businesses has grown to be a million-dollar enterprise.

ART B. USED LDC FUNDS TO RENEW
HIS RESTAURANT

A good case in point is that of Art B., an experienced restaurateur who'd been a part of the downtown Baltimore business community for more than three decades. When plans were made to renovate the area, Art knew that his fading restaurant could experience a renaissance if he came up with the funds to remodel it into a fancy French eatery. The estimates to raze his current structure and replace it with a dazzling new building were in excess of $600,000—far more than Art could come up with or even get the down payment for.

"Just when I thought all was lost," he notes, "I learned about the Local Development Corporations. These groups are absolute life savers for business owners like myself. I presented my plan to them, told how much money was needed and, lo and behold, they thought that my proposed Beaux Art restaurant would be an attractive addition to the community. They agreed to build the facility for me with their funds and let me pay it out on a schedule that I could handle with ease."

To make a long story short, Art's restaurant has been a smashing success. He does a tremendous lunch business with local executives and professionals, runs a busy bar from noon to midnight and hosts a packed tourist trade for dinner. "I'm making more money than I ever made in my life—clearing about half a million a year, I have the most beautiful restaurant in the state and I was smart enough to risk other people's money to get here."

LDCs generally process financing requests within two months of application. The request is then forwarded to the SBA which usually makes its decision within two weeks. Finally, bank reviews, when applicable, slow the process for another two to three weeks. Approach your local SBA office for details.

*   *   *   *   *   *

FINANCING FROM SBICs

• **Small Business Investment Companies.** In the never-ending quest for small business financing, persistence is the secret to success. The rule is simple: never leave a stone unturned. One of the better and richer sources of business loans is also one of the least known. It is the national network of Small Business Investment Companies (SBICs).

SBICs are privately-owned ventures licensed by the Small Business Administration to provide financial services to small firms. Nationwide, there are more than 250 SBICs representing an enormous amount of capital resources: total SBIC assets now exceed $1 billion. To date, SBICs have loaned more than $2.5 billion to more than 45,000 small companies.

Most important, this is a very good point in time to be exploring SBIC financing. Although previously committed to equity participation in high-flying growth companies, many SBICs have now widened their lending activities.

"Changes in the capital markets have forced many SBICs to do a good deal more straight lending than in the past," says a high-ranking official of the National Association of SBICs. "Small firms that may not have been considered exciting enough at one time to attract SBIC interest, may now find they can get the loans they need. There is money available for sound, well-managed companies."

To qualify for SBIC financing, most companies must be considered small businesses by SBIC current definitions. The standards for what are considered "small businesses" change from time to time. In a recent year, the guidelines were:

• Total assets under $9 million
• Average aftertax earnings less than $400,000 annually
• Net worth less than $4 million

As noted, these guidelines change—and there are exceptions to them—so companies interested in SBIC financing should check their nearest SBIC.

SBIC financing falls into two major categories: straight lending and equity participation. Loans are made from five to 20 years with interest rates ranging substantially above the current prime. Even at the higher rates, however, many small firms still find it beneficial to deal with SBICs. The reason is clear: long-term loans are often unavailable from banks.

"Small companies can get lower interest rates from the SBICs if they are willing to offer equity participation," says the SBIC official. "For companies with good growth prospects, the SBIC may be willing to lower the interest rate considerably. In this case, warrants may be attached to the loan, thus enabling the SBIC to buy into the company at a later date."

Remember, you are free to negotiate with the SBICs for the best possible deal. It's even a good idea to shop around, comparing the terms available from a number of SBICs. There are no geographical limitations: SBICs can make loans to firms in any part of the country. The best approach is to find the location of the nearest SBICs and set up appointments for initial discussions. A free directory of SBICs is available by writing to the National Association of SBICs, Washington Building, Washington, D.C. 20005.

Once you get your foot in the door, be well prepared to provide a detailed picture of your company. Most SBICs will want a general history of the firm, its products and markets; a profile of management; audited financial statements for the past five years; and projections for the use of borrowed funds. Remember, the more professional your presentation, the better your chances of securing the required funds. The effort is worth it: SBICs can make loans for up to $7.5 million.

*   *   *   *   *   *

MINORITY ENTERPRISE SMALL BUSINESS INVESTMENT COMPANIES

• **MESBICs.** Similar to the traditional SBICs. MESBICs are geared especially for loans to small business people who are members of minority groups. The MESBICs have been established to fill the void in the capital markets for minority group members. Minorities account for about 20 percent of our national population, yet own less than five percent of the businesses. MESBICs are designed to help more minorities enter the mainstream of business ownership.

MESBICs are part of the SBIC program and come under the administration of the SBA. MESBICs are governed by much the same rules as SBICs but there are some important differences.

First, MESBICs invest only in ventures that are at least 50 percent owned and managed by members of minority and/or economically disadvantaged groups. Second, MESBICs are often "backed" by large corporations or active organizations which can provide substantial amounts of capital both to the MESBIC and its client companies.

A typical MESBIC financing involved a minority firm that wanted to embark on a path of substantial expansion. Its first objective was to acquire an existing company in the same field. The acquisition would require $200,000 but the firm only had $30,000 cash on hand for the deal. To make matters worse, all of the banks approached by management refused to come up with any part of the financing required. Finally, contacts were made with a local MESBIC which provided $140,000. Add to this the buyer's $30,000 and a seller's note for about $30,000 and the transaction was able to be completed.

MESBICs have also played major roles in the financing of films. The movie **Black Godfather**, financed by two West Coast MESBICs for $350,000, earned rentals in excess of $5.5 million.

MESBICs are most active in providing long-term loans, venture capital, and loan guarantees made by third parties. In addition to pure capital, MESBICs are also a good source of management assistance and financial information for minority-owned businesses just starting up or seeking to expand.

MESBICs like to make their initial investments in client companies in the form of debt instruments that provide some option for equity participation. Once MESBIC funds get a start-up company rolling or enable an existing firm to expand, management can turn to the MESBIC for traditional business loans on an ongoing basis (providing, of course, that the borrower satisfies the loan criteria).

Loan periods usually range anywhere from 30 days to ten years. In certain situations, arrangements may be worked out to postpone repayment of the loan principal until the company is in a relatively strong position. This can be of tremendous aid in helping a company get on its feet. MESBICs favor those investments promising an average annual rate of return of at least 20 percent. For the location of the nearest MESBIC, contact your local SBA office (check the white pages under U.S. Government listings) or write to the Office of Minority Business Enterprise, U.S. Commerce Department, Washington, D.C.

*   *   *   *   *   *

CLEAN UP WITH AN EPA LOAN

• **Environmental Protection Agency Loans.** The national campaign to clean up America is proving to be an expensive exercise for the small business community. Many entrepreneurs are trapped between tough environmental codes and the skyrocketing costs of achieving legal compliance.

One solution is to seek financial aid from the federal government. A low-cost loan program, administered by the Environmental Protection Agency (EPA) is now available to small companies. Owner-managers can obtain pollution abatement loans at reasonable interest rates and can take up to 30 years to repay. The availability of low-interest loans is a boon to small companies unable to attract private financing. It is increasingly true that one of the key responsibilities in running a business is the provision for pollution control facilities. More and more local, state and federal regulations require that existing firms stop polluting practices and that new firms provide for pollution measures before being granted building or operating permits.

In many cases, this translates into considerable expense. A new drainage system, waste management facilities or exhaust filtration devices can run up to $100,000 or more. Getting a long-term low-interest EPA loan can provide the cash for these purchases without tying up the company's capital. What's more, EPA loans are just one of the many types of available government and government-related loan programs we will be discussing. By tapping as many of these sources as possible, the business owner is putting the technique of leveraging to use for its fullest potential.

Owner-managers interested in applying for pollution abatement loans may write to the Environmental Protection Agency, East Tower, 401 M. Street, Washington, D.C. 20460.

*   *   *   *   *   *

THE BIGGEST SOURCE OF
GOVERNMENT LOANS

• **Small Business Administration.** The biggest and most varied source for government loans is the Small Business Administration (SBA). Small manufacturers, wholesalers, retailers, service concerns, farmers and other businesses can borrow from the agency to construct, expand or convert facilities, purchase buildings, equipment, materials or obtain working capital.

By law, the agency can not make a loan if a business can obtain funds from a bank or other private source. You must, therefore, first seek private financing before applying to the SBA. If you live in a small city, you need apply to only one bank first; if you live in a city of 200,000 or more, you must try two banks before approaching the SBA. Although this may seem like an unnecessary bureaucratic procedure, it is actually a plus for the leveraged entrepreneurs. It means that when the banks close their doors on you—if that should happen—there is an alternate source of capital. Bear in mind that the SBA has an official directive from Congress to promote small business' contribution to our economy—to foster and stimulate companies like yours.

For business loan purposes, the SBA defines a small business as one that is independently owned and operated, not dominant in its field and meets the following standards:

• *Manufacturing*—The number of employees may not exceed 1500 (less for certain industries)

• *Wholesaling*—Annual sales must be between $9.5 and $22 million, depending on the types of merchandise involved.

• *Services*—Annual receipts must range between $2 and $8 million, depending on the industry in which the applicant is engaged.

• *Retailing*—Yearly sales should fall between $2 and $7.5 million.

- *Construction*—For general construction, average annual receipts can not exceed $9.5 million for the three most-recently completed fiscal years. Special trade construction loans require that these receipts not exceed $2 million.
- *Agriculture*—Annual receipts can not exceed $1 million.

(Local SBA offices can provide details on the precise standards for your specific business or merchandise category).

The general requirements for SBA loans include the following:

- Proof of good character.
- Show the ability to operate the business successfully.
- Have some prior capital so that, combined with the SBA loan, you can operate your venture on a sound financial footing.
- Be prepared to show that your past earnings record and the future prospects of your firm indicate the ability to repay the loan out of profits.

SBA financing takes many forms. The two most popular are bank guarantees and direct loans. When financing is not otherwise available on reasonable terms, the SBA can guarantee up to 90 percent or $350,000 ($500,000 in special situations), whichever is less, of a bank loan to a small firm. What happens here is that most of the risk of your loan shifts from the bank to the SBA, thus encouraging the bank to accept your application. The SBA stands behind you and guarantees most of the loan.

If the loan is still not available from a private lender, the SBA will consider advancing you funds on an immediate participation basis with a bank. Here, the SBA will come up with as much as $150,000. Failing all of this, the SBA may make a direct loan to you of up to $150,000.

SBA loans may be made for as long as 10 years, except those portions of loans used to acquire real property or construction facilities, where the maturity is 20 years. Working capital loans are often limited to 6 years.

Interest rates on the SBA's portion of immediate participations, as well as direct loans, may not exceed a rate set by a statutory formula relating to the cost of money to the Government. Within certain limitations, the bank sets the interest rate on guaranteed loans and its portion of immediate participation loans.

Collateral for SBA loans may consist of one or more of the following: a mortgage on land, a building and/or equipment; assignment of warehouse receipts for marketable merchandise; a mortgage on chattels; guarantees or personal endorsements, and in some instances, assignment of current receivables.

SBA loans cover a broad scope of business needs and requirements. In addition to the standard SBA loans, there are the following specialized programs:

Seasonal Lines of Credit

These are made to companies with seasonal loan requirements. Borrowers must have been in operation for at least a year before the loan application is made. Amounts range up to $500,000 and the money is expected to be used to increase working capital. These loans can be especially helpful to leveraged entrepreneurs in highly-seasonal businesses such as apparel, toys and fuel oil. About $40 million worth of these credit lines are granted yearly.

Contract Loan Program

This program is designed for small construction contractors or manufacturing or servicing industries who provide a specific product or service under an assignable contract. Allows up to $500,000 and matures in no longer than 18 months from date of first disbursement.

Displaced Business Loans

These loans are for economic injury caused to companies by Federally (or state of local) assisted construction projects. There is no dollar limit on these loans and interest rates are well below prime for the SBA's share. Maturity is in 30 years. The beauty of this program is that any business damage done to your firm as a result of government construction projects can be rectified with government money.

Handicapped Assistance Loans

These loans are available to nonprofit organizations and workshops working with the handicapped and to small companies owned 100 percent by handicapped individuals. The maximum amount of a loan is $350,000 for up to 15 years. The SBA can guarantee up to 90 percent, not to exceed $350,000, of a loan made by a private lending organization. Direct loans from the SBA are limited to $100,000, except in unusual circumstances, but are made at very low interest rates. The borrower must indicate the ability to repay the loan; proof of handicap alone is not sufficient for approval by any means. The program does, however, help the handicapped get financing for business growth and development, providing they have some business expertise or track record. Every handicapped individual with even some of these qualifications should at least try for one of these loans. About $17 million worth of these loans are made in a given year.

Physical Disaster Loans

These loans for businesses are available in an area deemed to have suffered a major physical disaster by the SBA or by the President of the U.S. If your business facilities are damaged during such official disasters, SBA loans are available to restore them, as nearly as possible, to predisaster condition. This includes inventory, furniture, fixtures, machinery, equipment and leasehold improvements.

Maturity ranges up to 30 years, with payments usually required monthly; the first payment is ordinarily due within five months of disbursement. A key point about Physical Disaster Loans is that the SBA does not require applicants to pay disaster expenses from his personal resources before obtaining a disaster loan.

Loans are available for up to $500,000 but can not exceed the actual tangible loss suffered by the disaster victim. The SBA does not require collateral for disaster loans.

Loans to Builders

These loans are made to those general contractors with annual receipts of less than $9.5 million. Up to $350,000 is available to construct new residential or commercial properties or to rehabilitate existing structures, for immediate resale on their own account.

Interest rates vary according to market conditions. For new construction, loan money may be used only for labor and materials.

The SBA requires evidence that there will be a market for the type of structure being built or rehabilitated and that permanent mortgage money is available in the area where the property is located.

Economic Opportunity Loans

These loans available to any resident of the U.S., Puerto Rico and Guam whose total family income from all sources is not sufficient for the basic needs of that family; or due to social or economic disadvantage if the applicant has been denied the opportunity to acquire adequate business financing through normal lending channels on reasonable terms.

Every applicant must, however, demonstrate the ability to operate a business successfully. There must also be reasonable assurance that the loan can be repaid from the earnings of the business. And while character is considered to be more important than collateral for these types of loans, applicants are expected to have some money or other assets invested in the business. This loan program provides for both financial and management assistance. The maximum amount of an EOL loan is $100,000 for up to 15 years.

Occupational Safety and Health Loan Program

This program is authorized to assist any small business concern that must make changes in its equipment, facilities or methods of operation in order to comply with provisions of the Occupational Safety and Health Act, if the SBA determines that such a concern is likely to suffer substantial economic injury without a loan.

This is increasingly important because OSHA, as the law is called, is an example of sweeping legislation that can force small companies to spend several hundred thousand dollars or more just to comply with needed, and in most cases quite appropriate, worker safety standards. Proceeds of OSHA loans can be used for new construction, remodeling or renovation (including equipment), paying back loans used for such purposes or replacing to finance start-up costs and meet continuing fixed costs when operations are curtailed because of construction or changes in methods of operation.

There is no statutory limitation on the dollar amount of loans. However, direct loans and the SBA share of bank participation loans are limited to $500,000, except in cases of extreme hardship. Bank loans guaranteed by the SBA have no dollar limit in this case.

To apply for a loan, the applicant can be considered under one of two procedures:

Voluntary Compliance Procedure: when the firm proposes to independently initiate structural, operational or other changes in order to comply with federal standards, describing existing conditions intended to be corrected in compliance with OSHA standards.

Cited Violation Procedure: When a small business is required by OSHA to undertake action in order to meet federal standards as shown by a citation.

Keep these loans in mind. OSHA inspections of your place of business can come at any time, without warning. The tab for legal compliance may be high. OSHA loans can help to pay for this without depriving the venture of cash needed for growth strategies. Also, by seeking voluntary compliance loans you can improve worker safety, bolster employee morale and therefore develop a more productive work environment.

Surety Bond Guarantee Program

This program is of exceptional benefit to contractors required to have a bid, performance or payment bond in order to obtain a contract. Eligibility is for contract bonds for which there is a provision in the contract section of the rate manual of the Surety Association of America, which is required by the contract documents and which is executed by a surety company acceptable to the U.S. Treasury Department or a surety otherwise qualified by the SBA to participate in the Bond Guarantee Program.

The SBA can guarantee bonds for contracts up to $1 million and there is no limit on the number of bonds that can be guaranteed for any one contractor. In consideration of the Surety Company's paying the SBA 20 percent of the gross bond premium, SBA guarantees the Surety Company up to 90 percent of any loss sustained on contracts up to $250,000 or greater, subject to a $500 maximum deductible to the Surety Company regardless of the contract amount.

The bond guarantee program enables contractors in a variety of fields to compete for big jobs they might not ordinarily be able to qualify for. By using this program, most of the financial risk shifts to the SBA, not the contractor.

The cost of the SBA guarantee is borne by the contractor and the company:

1.   If the SBA agrees to provide the guarantee and prior to execution of the bond, the contractor must pay the SBA a fee of .2% ($2 per $1000) of the contract amount. The contractor must also pay the company a maximum premium charge for the bond which is 1 ½ percent ($15 per $1000) on the first $250,000 of contract amount and 1% ($10 per $1000) on the excess.

2.   When the bond is executed, the company must pay the SBA 20 percent of its premium charge on the bond.

Pool Loans

The SBA can provide substantial financial assistance to a group of eligible small firms through a single pool loan. A loan can be made to a corporation formed and capitalized by a group of small businesses interested in obtaining raw materials, equipment, inventories or supplies or the benefits of research and development for the use of their individual small businesses. A loan can also be made to a group that wants to establish facilities for such purposes.

The maximum amount of the pool loan is $250,000 for each firm in the group. For example, if 10 small firms were to incorporate, they could be eligible for a loan of $2.5 million. If a bank participates with the SBA, the total and individual amounts could go much higher.

Pool loans are repaid over a period of ten years except when the construction of facilities is involved. In such cases, the loan may be amortized over a 20-year period, plus time needed to complete construction.

To qualify, two or more small business concerns must form and capitalize the group corporation. The leveraged entrepreneur can use the pool loan technique to bolster his individual financing strategies. By working with a group, as well as independently, the business has a better opportunity to achieve outstanding growth through the power of shared research, distribution or marketing facilities.

The following is a review and summary of general SBA loan information as well as some common questions and answers about SBA activities:

Q.   WHAT IS THE SMALL BUSINESS ADMINISTRATION

A.   The Small Business Administration (SBA) is a permanent, independent government Agency created by Congress in 1953 to encourage, assist, and protect the interests of small businesses.

* * *

Q.   WHAT IS AN SBA GUARANTEED LOAN?

A.   It is a loan made by a private lender as authorized by the SBA pursuant to a guaranty agreement between SBA and the private lender. SBA can guarantee up to 90 percent, or $500,000 in exceptional cases, whichever is less, of a loan to a small business firm. The interest rate must be reasonable and is set by the lender within certain limits set by state law and maximum permissible rates published by SBA from time to time.

* * *

Q.   WHY DOES SBA GUARANTEE LOANS BY PRIVATE LENDING INSTITUTIONS?

A.   In order to make funds available to those small businesses which are unable to obtain the needed credit on reasonable terms from normal credit sources without the guaranty by the U.S. Government.

* * *

Q.   HOW GOOD IS THE GUARANTEE?

A.   The terms and conditions of SBA's guaranty are contained in the guaranteed loan participation agreement between SBA and the bank. The statutory authority for SBA to guarantee loans to small business concerns is provided in Section 7 of the Small Business Act. The Attorney Generals of the United States have repeatedly rendered opinions that guarantees by a Federal Agency pursuant to valid statutory authority are secured by the full faith and credit of the United States Government.

* * *

Q.   WHAT IS THE AVERAGE SIZE OF AN SBA GUARANTEED BANK LOAN?

A.   In the area of $70,000 to $80,000 on regular business loans, but an individual loan guaranty may be as high as $500,000, in exceptional cases, or 90 percent, whichever is less.

* * *

Q.   ARE ALL SBA GUARANTEED LOANS ISSUED AT THE SAME INTER-
     EST RATE?

A.   No. SBA requires that interest rates on loans that are guaranteed by
     SBA be legal and reasonable. The individual states have their own
     statutes with respect to the legality of interest rates, and SBA
     publishes from time to time the maximum rate it considers
     reasonable.

*   *   *

Q.   ARE SBA GUARANTEED LOANS LEGALLY QUALIFIED FOR
     INVESTMENT BY FIDUCIARIES, STATE AND LOCAL PENSION
     FUNDS, AND INSTITUTIONAL INVESTORS?

A.   State laws generally govern the authorized or permitted investments
     by pension funds, fiduciaries, insurance companies and so on. The
     loan portion guaranteed by SBA, being a United States Govern-
     ment guaranty backed by the full faith and credit of the United
     States is generally accepted as an authorized investment in most
     states. Where there is any question, it is solved by getting an opinion
     from the appropriate State official.

*   *   *

Q.   IS THE SBA GUARANTY ASSIGNABLE?

A.   The guaranteed portion of an SBA loan may be assigned to a sec-
     ondary participant by the execution of secondary Participation
     Guaranty Agreement (SBA Form 1084) by the lender, the secondary
     participant, and SBA; subsequent transfers are made by notification
     pursuant to Form 1084. Assignments may otherwise be made under
     the Guaranty Agreement, SBA Form 750, but the rights and benefits
     under Form 1084 are only available if SBA executes Form 1084.

*   *   *

Q.   ON WHAT BASIS ARE PAYMENTS MADE ON SBA GUARANTEED
     LOANS?

A.   SBA loans are usually amortizing term loans providing for regular
     monthly payments of principal and interest.

*   *   *

Q.   WHY WOULD A LENDER WANT TO SELL THE GUARANTEED
     PORTION OF A SBA LOAN?

A.   To increase its earnings, and to generate the funds with which it
     makes additional financing in its community and accomodate the
     credit needs of additional customers.

*   *   *

	BUSINESS LOANS* Direct, Immediate Participation and Guaranty Loans	ECONOMIC OPPORTUNITY LOANS* Direct, Immediate Participation and Guaranty Loans
WHO IS ELIGIBLE?	Most businesses including farms that are: (1) independently owned and operated and not dominant in their fields; (2) unable to obtain private financing on reasonable terms; (3) qualified as "small" under SBA's size standards, based on dollar volume of business or number of employees.	Low income or disadvantaged persons who have lacked the opportunity to start or strengthen a small business and cannot obtain the necessary financing from other sources on reasonable terms.
LOAN PURPOSES	Business construction, conversion or expansion, purchase of equipment, facilities, machinery, supplies or materials and working capital.	Any use which will carry out the purposes shown above, generally, the same as other business loans.
MAXIMUM AMOUNT	$350,000** to any one borrower is the maximum SBA share of an immediate participation loan, where SBA and private lending institution each put up part of loan funds immediately; and the maximum SBA direct loan, one made by the Agency. For guaranteed loans, made by a bank and partially guaranteed by SBA, the maximum is also $350,000 normally but may be up to $500,000 for exceptional circumstances.	$100,000 to any one borrower, as SBA share of loan.

*Under the Handicapped Assistance Loan Program. financial aid is available to handicapped individuals to start or operate small firms, and to nonprofit organizations which employ the handicapped to make a product or provide service. Further details at local SBA office.

**At times, SBA may have lower ceilings in order to conserve limited funds.

66

	BUSINESS LOANS* (Cont.) Direct, Immediate Participation and Guaranty Loans	ECONOMIC OPPORTUNITY LOANS* (Cont.) Direct, Immediate Participation and Guaranty Loans
INTEREST RATE	6⅝ per annum on direct loan and SBA share of an immediate participation loan. On the bank's share of an immediate participation loan, the lending institution may set reasonable and legal rate with a maximum ceiling set by SBA from time to time. On a guaranty loan, bank may set legal and reasonable rate, with a maximum ceiling set by SBA from time to time.	On direct loans and SBA share of immediate participation loans, the rate is set periodically, based on a statutory formula. Bank rate same as on other business loans.
MATURITY	Maximum of 10 years as a rule. However, working capital loans generally are limited to 6 years, while portions of loans for construction and acquisition of real estate may have maximum of 20 years.	Maximum of 15 years, Working capital loans generally limited to a 10-year maximum.
TYPE OF COLLATERAL	Real estate or chattel mortage; assignment of warehouse receipts for marketable merchandise; assignment of certain types of contracts; guarantees or personal endorsements; in some instances assignment of current receivables.	Any worthwhile collateral which is available or will be acquired with the proceeds of the loan.

*Under the Handicapped Assistance Loan Program, financial aid is available to handicapped individuals to start or operate small firms, and to nonprofit organizations which employ the handicapped to make a product or provide service. Further details at local SBA office.

STATE AND LOCAL DEVELOPMENT COMPANY LOANS

	State Development Companies	Local Development Companies
WHO IS ELIGIBLE?	Any corporation organized under or pursuant to a special Act of the State Legislature, with authority to operate statewide and to assist the growth and development of business concerns, including small businesses, in its area.	Any corporation which: (a) is formed by public-spirited citizens interested in planned economic growth of a community with at least 75 percent ownership and control held by persons living or doing business in the community; (b) has been incorporated either for profit or non-profit under laws of the State in which it expects to do business; (c) is authorized to promote and assist the growth and development of small businesses in its area of operations; and (d) has a minimum of 25 stockholders or members.
LOAN PURPOSES	To help State development company provide equity capital and long-term loans to small business.	To help a development company acquire land and building; construct a new plant; purchase necessary machinery and equipment; expand or convert an existing plant, provided the project will assist a specific small business.
MAXIMUM AMOUNT	As much as State development company's total outstanding borrowings from all other sources. Based on experience, the average loan request from a State development company is $500,000 to $1,000,000. (Total available limited by annual budget allocations).	$500,000 for each identifiable small business to be assisted . . . as a prerequisite to obtaining SBA financing, a development company must provide a reasonable share of cost of project in funds raised by sale of stock, debentures, memberships, or cash equivalent (e.g., land). Minimum amount to be provided by development company will generally be 20 percent of cost of project. SBA will take a second lien position when the local lending institutions will participate in the SBA's first mortgage plan.

STATE AND LOCAL DEVELOPMENT COMPANY LOANS (Cont.)

	State Development Companies	Local Development Companies
SOURCE OF LOAN FUNDS	Direct from SBA.	(a) Bank loan guaranteed by SBA to 90 percent of the loan or $500,000 whichever is the lesser; (b) Bank loan with immediate participation by SBA; (c) Bank First Mortgage loan and SBA direct second mortgage loan; or (d) Direct from SBA.
INTEREST RATE	Published annually.	(a) Guaranteed loans: legal and reasonable rate on entire loan balance; (b) immediate participation; legal and reasonable rate on bank share and published rate on SBA share; (c) First mortgage; legal and reasonable rate on bank loan, published rate on SBA loan; (d) Direct SBA loan; published rate.
MATURITY	Maximum 20 years. In actual practice, these loans are usually requested for a 5 to 10 year term.	Maximum maturity of 25 years plus estimated time required to complete construction, conversion or expansion. Usually 15 to 20 years.
TYPE OF COLLATERAL	Security for SBA loan on an equal basis with funds borrowed by development company from any other sources after August 21, 1958. (SBA funds may be secured on a ratable basis with other borrowings of the State development company.)	A lien on the fixed assets acquired with loan proceeds so as to reasonably assure repayment of the loan.

69

LOANS TO SMALL BUSINESS INVESTMENT COMPANIES

and

LICENSEES ORGANIZED SOLELY TO ASSIST DISADVANTAGED ENTREPRENEURS

WHO IS ELIGIBLE	A regular small business investment company (SBIC) or small business investment company organized under Section 301(d) of the SBA Act, solely to assist disadvantaged entrepreneurs. Although statutory minimum capital is less, SBA, by policy, requires a minimum capital of at least $500,000. An SBIC must show that such capital is adequate to operate actively and profitably. A Section 301(d) Licensee with limited capital must show that funds will be provided to cover its operating expenses without depleting its capital.
LOAN PURPOSES	To provide an SBIC or Section 301(d) SBIC with funds for financing eligible small business for their growth, modernization, and/or expansion.
MAXIMUM AMOUNT	An SBIC is eligible to borrow $3 for every $1 of private capital up to a maximum of $35 million. An SBIC which has 65 percent or more of its total funds available invested in venture capital is eligible to borrow $4 for every $1 of its private capital, up to a total maximum of $35 million, provided it has private capital of $500,000 or more. The same eligibility applies to Section 301(d) Licensees, except that the required venture capital investment is 30 percent and there is no limit on funding.

70

LOANS TO SMALL BUSINESS INVESTMENT COMPANIES (Cont.)

INTEREST RATE	SBA provides the authorized leverage funds to an SBIC through its 100 percent guarantee of the debentures sold to the Federal Financing Bank. Debentures sold to the Federal Financing Bank bear interest at comparable Agency rates for paper of a similar maturity. Section 301(d) SBIC debentures sold to SBA bear interest at a rate not less than a rate determined by the Secretary of Treasury plus any additional charge toward covering other costs of the program which SBA may determine consistent with its purpose. Section 301(d) SBICs are eligible for a subsidized interest rate for the first five years on their debentures sold to SBA, subject to repayment of that subsidy before any distribution is made to stockholders other than SBA.
MATURITY	Maximum 15 years.
SECURITY	Evidence of indebtedness is a debenture of the SBIC or Section 301(d) Licensee subordinated to any debenture bonds, promissory notes, or other debts and obligations of the SBIC or Section 301(d) SBIC unless the SBA, in the exercise of reasonable investment prudence, determines otherwise. Adequately capitalized Section 301(d) Licensees are eligible for SBA purchases of their 3% cumulative preferred stock in an amount equivalent to a portion or all of their paid-in capital and paid-in surplus, the proceeds thereof constituting a part of their authorized leverage.

71

DISASTER LOANS

| | PHYSICAL DISASTER | | | ECONOMIC INJURY | |
	Storms, Floods, etc.	Natural Causes & Diseased Products	Displaced Business	Compliance	Economic Impact
WHO IS ELIGIBLE?	Individuals, businesses, nonprofit organizations such as churches provided: (a) they have suffered tangible property loss from a disaster and; (b) SBA has declared their area a disaster loan area.	Any small business located in area of physical or natural disaster as determined by the President, SBA, or Secretary of Agriculture, provided business has suffered substantial economic injury or, as determined by SBA from inability to process or market a product of human consumption because of disease or toxicity from natural or undetermined causes, including livestock and poultry raisers in the event of animal disease.	Any small business suffering substantial economic injury as a result of displacement by, or proximity to, urban renewal, highway, or other federally-aided, or State or local construction projects.	Any small business judged to have suffered substantial economic injury caused by complying with Federal health, safety, food processing, air and water pollution, and other federal regulations.	Any small business judged to have suffered substantial economic injury caused by 1) closing of a major military installation, 2) reduction of Federal support of projects as result of international agreements limiting strategic arms, 3) emergency energy shortages, and 4) economic dislocation

72

DISASTER LOANS (Cont.)

| | PHYSICAL DISASTER | | | ECONOMIC INJURY | |
	Storms, Floods, etc.	Natural Causes & Diseased Products	Displaced Business	Compliance	Economic Impact
LOAN PURPOSES	To restore a home, business or nonprofit institution to pre-disaster condition. For repair and replacement of real estate, furnishings, equipment, fixtures and inventory. For refinancing, if the uninsured damage exceeds 30% of the pre-disaster value of the property.	Working capital and payment of financial obligations (except long-term bank loans) which small business could have met had it not suffered revenue loss because of disaster conditions. To reestablish or continue a small firm injured economically by diseased products.	To help firm obtain comparable space. For purchase of land and buildings, moving expenses, replacement of machinery and equipment, increased rent, inventory, working capital, etc.	To help firm meet standards by upgrading plant or equipment Proceeds of loan can be used for working capital only under certain conditions.	Generally, to help firm to continue in business and overcome the economic injury sustained.
MAXIMUM AMOUNT	For business, direct or immediate participation including refinancing, $500,000 limit, SBA share, guaranteed loans, no dollar limit, up to 90% guarantee. For homes, direct or immediate participation, $50,000 structural damage; $10,000 furniture and personal effects; combined limit $55,000 maximum refinancing; guaranteed loans, no dollar limit, up to 90% SBA guarantee.	Determined by economic loss suffered by applicant as result of disaster and cost of reestablishment or continuation for diseased products economic injury. Same limits as Physical Disaster, either separately or combined with physical loss.	No dollar limit Loan is based on amount of economic injury sustained.	No dollar limit. Loan is based on amount of economic injury sustained.	No dollar limit. Loan is based on amount of economic injury sustained.

DISASTER LOANS (Cont.)

	PHYSICAL DISASTER			ECONOMIC INJURY	
	Storms, Floods, etc.	Natural Causes & Diseased Products	Displaced Business	Compliance	Economic Impact
INTEREST RATE	Statutory formula on direct loans and SBA's share of participation loans. Participating private lender may set reasonable rate on its share of immediate participation loan or on entire guaranty loan but not to exceed prevailing rate for regular SBA business loans.	Statutory formula for Direct and IP Loans; for guaranteed, same as physical disaster loans.	Set annually by statutory formula on SBA share of loans. Private lending institution may set reasonable interest rate on its share of loan, with a maximum ceiling set by SBA from time to time.	SBA share set annually by statutory formula. Banks may set a legal and reasonable rate with a maximum ceiling set by SBA from time to time.	SBA share set annually by statutory formula. Banks may set a legal and reasonable rate with a maximum ceiling set by SBA from time to time.
MATURITY	Maximum of 30 years.	Maximum of 30 years.	Maximum of 30 years.	Maximum of 30 years.	Maximum of 30 years.
TYPE OF COLLATERAL	No specific requirements Applicants must pledge whatever collateral is available.	No specific requirements. Whatever can be pledged must be. If fixed assets are acquired with proceeds of an SBA loan, they must be pledged. An assignment of any existing leases is required.	No specific requirements. Whatever can be pledged must be. If fixed assets are acquired with proceeds of an SBA loan they must be pledged. Refusal to pledge available collateral may be sufficient reason to decline.	Whatever can be pledged must be. If fixed assets are acquired with proceeds of an SBA loan these assets must be pledged Refusal to pledge available collateral may be sufficient reason to decline.	Whatever can be pledged must be. If fixed assets are acquired with proceeds of an SBA loan, these assets must also be pledged. Refusal to pledge available collateral may be sufficient reason to decline.

SBA FIELD OFFICES

ADDRESSES AND TELEPHONE NUMBERS

(TELEPHONE NUMBERS FOR PUBLIC USE ONLY)

CITY	STATE	ZIP CODE	ADDRESS	
Boston	Mass.	02114	150 Causeway St., 10th Floor	(617) 223-3224
Boston	Mass.	02114	150 Causeway St., 10th Floor	(617) 223-3224
Holyoka	Mass.	01040	302 High Street-4th Floor	(413) 536-8770
Augusta	Maine	04330	Federal Building, 40 Western Ave., Room 512	(207) 622-6171
Concord	N.H.	03301	55 Pleasant St., Room 213	(603) 224-4041
Hartford	Conn.	06103	One Financial Plaza	(203) 244-3600
Montpelier	Vt.	05602	Federal Building, 87 State St., Room 210	(802) 223-7472
Providence	R.I.	02903	57 Eddy St., Room 7th Fl	(401) 528-1000
New York	N.Y.	10007	26 Federal Plaza, Room 3214	(212) 264-1468
New York	N.Y.	10007	26 Federal Plaza, Room 3100	(212) 264-4355
Melville	N.Y.	11746	425 Broad Hollow Rd. Rm. 205	(516) 752-1626
Hato Rey	Puerto Rico	00919	Chardon and Bolivia Streets, PO Box 1915	(809) 763-6363
St. Thomas	Virgin Island	00801	U.S. Fed. Ofc. Bldg., Veterans Dr., Rm. 283	(809) 774-8530
Newark	N.J.	07102	970 Broad St., Room 1635	(201) 645-2434
Camden	N.J.	08104	1800 East Davis Street	(609) 757-5183
Syracuse	N.Y.	13202	Federal Building-Room 1073-100 South Clinton Street	(315) 423-5370
Buffalo	N.Y.	14202	111 West Huron St., Room 1311, Federal Building	(716) 842-3240
Elmira	N.Y.	14901	180 State Street-Rm. 412	(607) 733-4686
Albany	N.Y.	12210	99 Washington Ave., Twin Towers Bldg., Room 921	(518) 472-6300
Rochester	N.Y.	14614	Federal Building, 100 State Street	(716) 263-6700
Philadelphia	Bala Cynwyd, Pa.	19004	231 St. Asaphs Rd., 1 Bala Cynwyd Plaza, Suite 646 West Lobby	(215) 597-5888
Philadelphia	Bala Cynwyd, Pa.	19004	231 St. Asaphs Rd., 1 Bala Cynwyd Plaza, Suite 400 East Lobby	(215) 597-5888
Harrisburg	Pa.	17102	1500 North 2nd Street	(717) 782-3840
Wilkes-Barre	Pa.	18702	Penn Place, 20 N. Pennsylvania Ave.	(717) 826-6497
Wilmington	Del.	19801	844 King Street, Federal Building, Rm. 5207	(302) 571-6294
Baltimore	Towson Md.	21204	Oxford Bldg., 8600 LaSalle Road, Rm. 630	(301) 962-4392
Clarksburg	W. Va.	26301	109 North 3rd St., Room 301, Lowndes Building	(304) 623-5631
Charleston	W. Va.	25301	Charleston National Plaza, Suite 628	(304) 343-6181
Pittsburgh	Pa.	15222	Federal Building, 1000 Liberty Ave., Room 1401	(412) 644-2780
Richmond	Va.	23240	Federal Building, 400 North 8th St., Room 3015	(804) 782-2617
Washington	D.C.	20417	1030 15th St. N.W. Suite 250	(202) 655-4000
Atlanta	Ga.	30309	1375 Peachtree St., N.E.	(404) 881-4943
Atlanta	Ga.	30309	1720 Peachtree Street, N.W., 6th Floor	(404) 881-4325

SBA FIELD OFFICES (Cont.)

ADDRESSES AND TELEPHONE NUMBERS

CITY	STATE	ZIP CODE	ADDRESS	(TELEPHONE NUMBERS FOR PUBLIC USE ONLY)
Birmingham	Ala.	35205	908 South 20th St., Room 202	(205) 254-1344
Charlotte	N.C.	28202	230 S. Tryon Street	(704) 372-0711
Greenville	N.C.	27834	215 South Evans Street Rm. 206	(919) 752-3798
Columbia	S.C.	29201	1801 Assembly St., Room 131	(803) 765-5376
Jackson	Miss.	39201	Providence Capitol Bldg., Suite 690, 200 E. Pascagoula St.	(601) 969-4371
Biloxi	Miss.	39530	111 Fred Haise Blvd., Gulf Nat. Life Insurance Bldg. 2nd Floor	(601) 435-3676
Jacksonville	Fla.	32202	Federal Building, 400 West Bay St., Room 261, PO Box 35067	(904) 791-3782
Louisville	Ky.	40202	Federal Building, 600 Federal Pl., Room 188	(502) 582-5971
Miami	Coral Gables Fla.	33134	2222 Ponce De Leon Blvd., 5th Floor	(305) 350-5521
Tampa	Fla.	33602	1802 N. Trask Street, Suite 203	(813) 228-2594
Nashville	Tenn.	37219	404 James Robertson Parkway, Suite 1012	(615) 251-5881
Knoxville	Tenn.	37902	502 South Gay St., Room 307, Fidelity Bankers Building	(615) 637-9300
Memphis	Tenn.	38103	Federal Building, 167 North Main St., Room 211	(901) 521-3588
West Palm Beach	Fla.	33402	Federal Building, 701 Clematis St., Room 229	(305) 659-7533
Chicago	Ill.	60604	Federal Building, 219 South Dearborn St., Room 838	(312) 353-0355
Chicago	Ill.	60604	Federal Building, 219 South Dearborn St., Room 437	(312) 353-4528
Springfield	Ill.	62701	One North, Old State Capital Plaza	(217) 525-4416
Cleveland	Ohio	44199	1240 East 9th St., Room 317	(216) 522-4180
Columbus	Ohio	43215	34 North High Street, Tonti Bldg.	(614) 469-6860
Cincinnati	Ohio	45202	Federal Building, 550 Main St.	(513) 684-2814
Detroit	Mich.	48226	477 Michigan Ave., McNamara Building	(313) 226-6075
Marquette	Mich.	49855	540 W. Kaye Ave., Don H. Bottum University Center	(906) 225-1108
Indianapolis	Ind.	46204	575 North Pennsylvania St., Rm. 552 New Fed. Bldg.	(317) 269-7272
Madison	Wis.	53703	122 West Washington Ave., Room 713	(608) 252-5261
Milwaukee	Wis.	53233	735 West Wisconsin Ave., Room 690, Continental Bank Bldg	(414) 224-3941
Eau Claire	Wis.	54701	500 South Barstow St., Room B9AA, Fed. Off. Bldg. & U.S. Courthouse	
Minneapolis	Minn.	55402	12 South 6th St., Plymouth Building	(715) 834-9012
Dallas	Tex.	75242	1720 Regal Row, Regal Park Office Bldg. Rm 3C36	(612) 725-2362
Dallas	Tex.	75670	1100 Commerce St., Room 300	(214) 749-2531
Marshall	Tex.	75670	100 South Washington Street, Federal Building G 12	(214) 749-3961
Albuquerque	N. Mex.	87110	5000 Marble Ave., N.E., Patio Plaza Bldg.	(505) 766-3430
Houston	Tex.	77002	One Allen Ctr., 500 Dallas Street	(713) 226-4341

SBA FIELD OFFICES (Cont.)

ADDRESSES AND TELEPHONE NUMBERS

CITY	STATE	ZIP CODE	ADDRESS	(TELEPHONE NUMBERS FOR PUBLIC USE ONLY)
Little Rock	Ark.	72201	611 Gaines St., Suite 900	(501) 378-5871
Lubbock	Tex.	79401	1205 Texas Ave., 712 Federal Office Bldg. & U.S. Courthouse	(806) 762-7011
El Paso	Tex.	79901	4100 Rio Bravo, Suite 300	(915) 543-7200
Lower Rio Grande Valley	Harlingen, Tex,	78550	222 East Van Buran Street	(512) 423-3011
Corpus Christi	Tex.	78408	3105 Leopard St.	(512) 888-3011
New Orleans	La.	70113	1001 Howard Ave., Plaza Tower, 17th Floor	(504) 589-2611
Shreveport	La.	71101	Fannin Street, U.S. Post Office & Courthouse Building	(318) 226-5196
Oklahoma City	Okla.	73102	Fed. Bldg., 200 N.W. 5th St., Suite 670	(405) 231-4301
San Antonio	Tex.	78206	727 E. Durango, Rm A 513	(512) 229-6250
Kansas City	Mo.	64106	911 Walnut St., 23rd Floor	(816) 374-3318
Kansas City	Mo.	64106	1150 Grande Ave. 5th Floor	(816) 374-5557
Des Moines	Iowa	50309	New Federal Building, 210 Walnut St., Room 749	(515) 284-4422
Omaha	Neb.	68102	Nineteenth and Farnum Streets, Empire State Building	(402) 221-4691
St Louis	Mo.	63101	Suite 2500, Mercantile Tower, One Mercantile Center	(314) 425-4191
Wichita	Kan.	67202	110 East Waterman Street, Main Place Building	(316) 267-6311
Denver	Colo.	80202	Executive Tower Bldg. 1405 Curtis Street, 22nd Floor	(303) 837-0111
Denver	Colo.	80202	721 19th St., Room 426A	(303) 837-0111
Casper	Wyo.	82601	Federal Building, Room 4001, 100 East B St.	(307) 265-5550
Fargo	N. Dak.	58102	Federal Building, 653 2nd Ave., North, Room 218	(701) 237-5131
Helena	Mont.	59601	618 Helena Avenue	(406) 449-5381

SBA FIELD OFFICES (Cont.)

ADDRESSES AND TELEPHONE NUMBERS

CITY	STATE	ZIP CODE	ADDRESS	(TELEPHONE NUMBERS FOR PUBLIC USE ONLY)
Salt Lake City	Utah	84138	Federal Building, 125 South State St., Room 2237	(801) 524-5800
Sioux Falls	S. Dak.	57102	National Bank Building, 8th & Main Ave., Room 402	(605) 336-2980
Rapid City	S. Dak.	57701	515 9th St., Federal Bldg., (Room) 246	(605) 343-5074
San Francisco	Calif.	94102	450 Golden Gate Ave., Box 36044	(415) 556-7487
San Francisco	Calif.	94105	211 Main Street	(415) 556-7490
Fresno	Calif.	93721	Federal Building, 1130 O St., Room 4015	(209) 487-5000
Sacramento	Calif.	95825	2800 Cottage Way	(916) 484-4726
Las Vegas	Nev.	89101	301 E. Stewart	(702) 385-6011
Reno	Nev.	89505	50 South Virginia St., Rm 308	(702) 784-5234
Honolulu	Hawaii	96813	1149 Bethel St., Room 402	(808) 546-8950
Agana	Guam	96910	Ada Plaza Center Building	( ) 777-8420
Los Angeles	Calif.	90071	350 S. Figueroa St., 6th Floor	(213) 688-2956
Phoenix	Ariz.	85004	112 North Central Ave.	(602) 261-3611
San Diego	Calif.	92188	880 Front Street, Federal U.S. Building, Room 4 S 33	(714) 293-5444
Seattle	Wash.	98104	710 2nd Ave., 5th Floor, Dexter Horton Building	(206) 442-1455
Seattle	Wash.	98174	915 Second Ave., Federal Building, Room 1744	(206) 442-5534
Anchorage	Alaska	99501	1016 West 6th Ave., Suite 200, Anchorage Legal Center	(907) 272-5561
Fairbanks	Alaska	99701	50½ Second Avenue	(907) 452-1951
Boise	Idaho	83702	216 North 8th St., Room 408	(208) 384-1096
Portland	Oreg.	97204	1220 S.W. Third Avenue, Federal Building	(503) 221-2682
Spokane	Wash.	99210	Court House Building, Room 651	(509) 456-3777

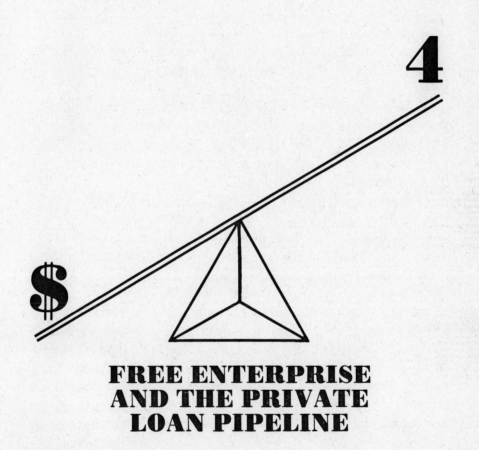

FREE ENTERPRISE AND THE PRIVATE LOAN PIPELINE

As I have noted, capital fires this nation's economy. It is the very foundation of free enterprise: the lubricant that keeps the business machine humming. Since the system is dependent on supplies of available capital, a great number of capital sources exist for those with a legitimate need. You have already explored some of these sources; you will discover many more.

The important point to remember—and this cannot be stressed enough—is that if you are starting, managing or expanding a business, there is ample capital available in this great economy of ours to satisfy your needs. It is the nature of the system. Without this assurance, the financial world would dry up in a matter of weeks. Knowing your way around the rich capital markets is a key to success in leveraged finance—and that's what I will help you do.

Too many small businesses suffer from a case of "capital myopia." That is, when it comes to borrowing money for business needs, they think in terms of only one category of loans. Just like those who focus only on the Small Business Administration for government loans, there are others who look to the federal government as the sole source for business financing. Although, as we have seen, the government can be a good source for loans, it is not the only show in town—far from it.

The free enterprise system itself has its own "Private Loan Pipeline," which, in many cases, is better than the government programs. Here, the amounts of money available are unlimited (into the millions of dollars), the requirements extremely flexible and the payment terms open to individual negotiations rather than hard and fast rules.

Most important, the private loan pipeline does not fluctuate according to political currents. Unlike federal loan programs, funding does not go up one year and then nosedive the next simply because of a bureaucratic economy drive. Private loan sources are a year-in—year-out fact of life. Part of the reason for this is that there is profit to be made in lending investment capital. Private capital sources are not in business for their health or for the public good. They operate to make a buck—and as long as the profit motive exists there will be private capital available to leverage business ventures like yours.

The range of good private capital sources is wide. Perhaps the fastest, simplest and least-complicated to use is the so-called Executive Credit. For those instances when you need quick infusions of capital of up to $25,000, Executive Credit can deliver in about a week and you'll never even have to leave your home or office. Just fill out a coupon and an application and the entire procedure is done by mail. If confidentiality is important, this is the route for you. No one will see you in a bank office; no one will have to know of your loan except the lender.

More than 20 companies now offer loan-by-mail services to businessmen and women across the nation. Some are small independent outfits; others are subsidiaries of large banks and finance companies. Most advertise their services in daily newspapers, business journals, trade publications and yellow pages and all will make loans to approved applicants anwhere in the U.S.

Mail loan repayment terms range from one to five years depending on the borrower's preference. Most lenders offer flexible terms to suit differing financial needs and many allow prepayment without penalty. This means you can make advance payments on the loans without incurring extra finance charges.

One well-known Executive Loan Source is:

Dial Financial Corp
1505 E. 17th St.
Santa Ana, California 92701   714-835-4774

"I spotted a great opportunity to sign up a new customer: a big new auto assembly plant," says Barton G., owner of a rapidly expanding factory cleaning and maintenance service in Trenton, New Jersey. "All I had to do was act fast and impress the plant's top brass that my outfit INDUSTRACLEAN could do the job.

"The problem was, the new plant was located near Newark and although we had rented office space there to tap that section of the New Jersey market, the office was not yet furnished. I knew I could make the best impression on the potential new customer if I could point to an established office near his facility."

So Barton acted fast. Rather than tampering with his major credit source at a local bank, he filed an application with a loan-by-mail outfit and got a check for the $12,300 needed to furnish the office in nine days.

"We picked furniture from stock, had it installed in less than a day and held our meeting with the plant executives in our luxuriously appointed office. As a result, we had the account in our pockets and signed the contract before lunch."

THE BIGGEST SOURCE OF PRIVATE
LOANS—BANK FINANCING

Of all the private pipeline loan sources, banks are the biggest, hands down. In practice, they make more loans by number, and for a greater dollar amount, than any other type of financial institution. The importance of the banks is illustrated by the SBA's official policies: since they consider the banks to be the nation's first line of financing, SBA officers can not consider your government loan requests until you have been rejected by the banks.

When we discuss banks as sources of money we are not, however, referring to any single, uniform procedure. Banks vary in the kinds of financing available, in the interest rates charged, in their willingness to accept risks and in their attitude towards small businesses. As a successful leveraged entrepreneur, you must understand these distinctions. It is your responsibility to size up a bank, to approach those most likely to authorize your loan, to know how to present your request in a professional manner and to identify the type of bank financing most suited to your business needs.

Let's review some of the essential basics of bank operations:

Banks generally offer four different types of financing: short, intermediate and long-term loans as well as lines of credit. Keep in mind that the purpose for which the funds are to be used is an important factor in deciding the kind of money needed. Different types of loans carry different interest rates, payment terms and other conditions. Getting the wrong kind of financing can make the money completely unsuitable for your business requirements: it may cost too much in terms of debt service and may have to be repaid too quickly. A very important distinction between the types of money available is how it must be repaid. Generally, short-term loans are repaid from the liquidation of current assets which they have financed. Long-term loans are generally repaid from earnings.

You can use short-term bank loans (less than a year) for purposes such as financing accounts receivable for a month or more. Or you can use them for applications that take longer to pay off—such as building a seasonal inventory over a period of five or six months. Usually, lenders expect short-term loans to be repaid after their purposes have been served: for example, accounts receivable loans, when the outstanding accounts have been paid by the borrowers customers, and inventory loans, when the inventory has been converted into saleable merchandise. Remember, that's all a leveraged entrepreneur needs the money for: you have used the funds of others to generate cash for yourself.

Banks grant this type of money in one of two ways: either on your general credit reputation with an unsecured loan or on a secured loan, which means collateral is put up. The unsecured loan is the most frequently-used form of bank credit for short-term purposes. You do not have to put up collateral because the bank relies on your credit reputation. This is one reason why it is always best to implement your leveraged strategies using at least one bank as your central lending institution. By taking loans, repaying them on schedule and proving yourself to be a competent business owner, the bank will favor you with special privileges, will make it easier for you to get money and will value you as a customer. To foster this kind of relationship, it is also a good idea to keep your company's accounts at the bank. Banks like to know that they are dealing with full-service customers.

I recently witnessed the power of good banking relationships first hand. On the same day in the same bank, two business owners approached the manager for loans. The first, who had never dealt with the bank before, was told that they were not currently in the loan market. "The capital situation is so tight at the moment," the manager said," that we are holding off on any new loans for the immediate future."

Not 20 minutes later, Alfred K., an extremely successful and high-leveraged home builder—who had always made it clear to the bank that he gave them all of his business, not just loans—approached the manager with the same loan query. This time, the conversation went like this:

Alfred: "Walter, I need another line of credit for $1.2 million. I'm going to develop 16 lots over on Dade Hill.

Walter (bank manager): Good choice. That's one hell of a beautiful location. So, $1.2 mill, ha. I see no reason why that can't be arranged. You know there's always a welcome mat here for customers like you Alfred. Now, let's do some paperwork on this. Just how . . . ."

Without this kind of personal banking relationship, you will required to put up a pledge of some or all of your assets. Among the various types of security pledges banks require for secured loans are:

Endorsers, Co-makers and Guarantors

Borrowers often get other people to sign a note in order to bolster their own credit. These endorsers are contingently liable for the note they sign. If the borrower fails to pay up, the bank expects the endorser to make the note good. Sometimes the endorser may be asked to pledge assets or securities that he owns.

As a leveraged entrepreneur, especially one just starting out, you may want to convince an established business owner to be your endorser. The best way to get another party to take this risk is to identify those companies or individuals who stand to benefit most by your success. Promise to deal only with a single supplier and prove that you will soon be a major customer and you may get that needed endorsement.

A co-maker is one who makes an obligation jointly with the borrower. In such cases, the bank can collect directly from either the maker or the co-maker. A guarantor is one who guarantees the payment of a note by signing a guaranty commitment. Sometimes, a manufacturer will act as a guarantor for one of his customers.

Assignment of Leases

The assigned lease as security is similar to the guarantee. The bank lends the money on a building and takes a mortgage. This is often used in franchising: the lease, which the dealer and the parent franchise company work out, is assigned so that the bank automatically receives the rent payments. In this manner, the bank uses its money to provide the building and is automatically assured repayment of the loan.

Accounts Receivable

Many banks lend money on accounts receivable. What this means, in effect, is that you are letting your customers pay off your note. The bank may take accounts receivable on a notification or a non-notification plan. Under the notification plan, the purchaser of the goods is informed by the bank that his account has been assigned to it and he is asked to pay the bank. Under the non-notification plan, the borrower's customers continue to pay him the sums due on their accounts and he pays the bank.

Chattel Mortgages

If you buy equipment such as a cash register or a truck, you may want to get a chattel mortgage loan. You give the bank a lien on the equipment you are buying.

Life Insurance

Another kind of collateral is life insurance. Banks will lend up to the cash value of a life insurance policy. You have to assign the policy to the bank. If the policy is on the life of an executive of a small corporation, corporate resolutions must be made authorizing the assignment. Most insurance companies allow you to sign the policy back to the original beneficiary when the assignment to the bank ends. It is often preferable to use life insurance as collateral rather than to borrow directly from insurance companies. One reason is that a bank loan is often more convenient to obtain and can often be obtained at a lower interest rate. Check out both options.

Other common forms of collateral are savings accounts, stocks and bonds and real estate holdings.

Most bank loans which extend beyond the short-term category must be secured. This longer-term borrowing provides you with money to be paid back over more than a year. There are intermediate-term loans, which are made from between one and five years and long-term loans, which are for more than five years. Both are the kinds of loans you will need to achieve major expansion; they are ordinarily repaid in periodic installments from earnings.

The best things about bank financing are that there is no set limit on how much you can borrow and, equally important, there are so many banks in and around every community that the persistent entrepreneur is more than likely to come up with a cooperative loan source. Count banks as extremely important in your leverage strategy. (We will have much more revealing information in future chapters on how to find the right banks and get them to work with you.)

COMMERCIAL FACTORS

Commercial factoring, one of the oldest forms of business financing, is another excellent way to get fast cash for business operations. Factoring uses the technique of professional money management to shore-up cash flow and to lubricate the financial wheels.

Let's say that you are faced with a familiar but exasperating business problem: many of your accounts are late or delinquent payers. Stubborn collection problems such as these can dry up cash flow, crippling your firm's operations. With so much money outstanding, you may not have the needed cash for growth stategies—for the steps necessary to expand your own business. Factoring, however, can help you raise cash and overcome this problem. To use factoring, you send all sales invoices directly to a commercial factor, who promptly reimburses you for up to 80 percent of the invoice values. The remaining balance is settled by the factor on the average collection date.

The beauty of it is that you are getting most of the money up front—you don't have to hold hands with delinquent accounts. The factor assumes part of your business risks—and as a leveraged entrepreneur, that's exactly what you want. Although factoring is an excellent technique for use by small firms, it is also employed by the corporate giants as well. Even some of the Fortune 500 turn to factoring when they need fast cash for their receivables.

As part of the service package, factors also prepare sales ledgers, implement and maintain credit controls and manage the client's collection efforts. In addition, many factors offer full credit insurance for approved debtors. This vital protection lends further strength to cash flow and can be particularly valuable for overseas transactions where customer's credit ratings are not easily ascertained.

Factors can serve as a sort of accounting and credit control department for your firm. At a time when financial savvy is at a premium, factors provide the services many small firms need but cannot afford to support internally. Factors can keep you up-to-date, for example, on the age of all your debts at the end of each month. This permits you to monitor customer activities before fulfilling further orders. You'll be less likely to get stuck with delinquent accounts this way—less likely to find yourself in a cash bind.

For growing firms, factoring's key benefit is the assurance of available funds. Once sales have been made, cash is immediately available for a large percentage of the firm's receipts. For this service, factors generally charge the bank overdraft rate for all advances as well as an additional service fee. The exact rate depends on the amount of risk involved and the amount of accounting work required.

There are commercial factors operating in virtually all major cities throughout the U.S. The best bet is to ask your banker or accountant for the name of a reputable factor in your area. Since many banks are now offering factoring as part of their services, your bank may bid to do the job itself. Among the better-known factors are:

1. Walter E. Heller & Co., Inc., 200 Park Ave., N.Y.C.
2. CIT Companies—Wm. Iselin & Co., 357 Park Ave. S., N.Y.C.

GETTING AROUND A LOAN OBSTACLE

• **Growth Capital Companies.** Sometimes, trying to arrange big league financing for small firms can be like trying to hit a home run with a toothpick. Some lenders do not want to make really substantial loans to small ventures. The problem is a classic "catch 22". Some financial institutions prefer to limit their major loans to big corporations. To get big, however, leveraged entrepreneurs need major cash infusions throughout the critical growth stages. The need for hefty loans develops well before your company can qualify as mature and fully developed.

Although this predicament can pose a major obstacle to the strategy of leveraged finance, there are ways to get around it. We have already explained how to make banks and other lenders more receptive to your needs—and we will provide more tips on this in later chapters. But another way to get around this "catch 22" is to detour traditional lenders (like banks) by turning to the so-called "growth capital companies" that have sprung up in recent years.

These outfits, which are often the business lending arms of commercial credit companies, do make million dollar loans to small firms.

"The companies we serve have as few as five employees and annual sales of as low as $100,000," says a vice president of Commercial Credit Capital Corp. "We make loans to them of from several hundred thousand dollars to several million and we offer payment terms of from three to ten years."

Growth capital outfits step in to fill the lending gap left by commercial bankers, government agencies and other cash sources when they shy away from making substantial loans to small companies. Growth capital loans are becoming increasingly popular with leveraged entrepreneurs. One reason is that they are flexible, enabling the borrower to repay, after the first three to five years, without penalty.

Growth capital funds may be used for a wide range of business projects including the acquisition of new equipment, building larger production facilities or purchasing another company in the same industry. Interest rates are geared to float at between three and six points above the prime rates (rates are generally lower for the larger loans).

In a typical transaction, a small manufacturing firm which was experiencing heavy demand for its products wanted to expand from a regional to a national market. To do so, the work force had to be doubled almost immediately. The owner borrowed about $1 million from a growth capital company, hired enough workers to put on a second shift and purchased additional production machinery. The firm surpassed its growth goals and was able to repay the loan well before the due date.

It must be pointed out, however, that growth capital loans are not available simply for the asking. No one lends up to $1 million or more without being fairly confident of the borrower's ability to repay. Although the criteria for these loans vary among the different lenders, the following guidelines are widely observed:

• Most of the growth capital companies demand that the loans be secured by some type of fixed assets. The value of the assets should be at least one and one-half times the amount of the loan.

• Projected cash flow must be more than enough to repay the loan. Here again, figure an amount equal to at least one and one-half the total required to retire the loan.

• Your management ability is also very important. The growth capital lenders must have faith in your ability to make the firm a success. You can win them over by demonstrating your abilities or your past track record.

"With a small amount of cash of my own, and a respectable loan of $53,000 from the Small Business Administration, I started a little plant making homemade ice cream," says Bob A. of Garden City, N.Y. "My unique selling point was to offer very unusual flavors, like apple, pumpkin and macadamia nut, that only I was selling. We sold our product under the Ice Cream Fantasy label to local diners, coffee shops, college campuses and ice cream parlors. Because of the unusual flavors and the high quality of the product, we could not keep up with demand. People seemed to want more and more Ice Cream Fantasy.' "

The turning point in Bob's business came when he recognized that the stores selling his product were cashing in big on the profits without doing very much to promote the product. By selling Ice Cream Fantasy through his own stores, Bob could do a better job of merchandising his brand, and even more important, could chalk up a higher profit.

"The problem was, I needed a cool $1.8 million to open enough stores to make my plan work—and I had nowhere near that kind of money. Three banks I approached gave me thumbs down because they said there were enough ice cream stores in the area. They didn't understand that my product concept made me different. I tried to explain that there were lots of hamburger places around before McDonald's got started, but my arguments fell on deaf ears.

"Then I learned of the growth capital outfits and I got a completely different reception there. They were willing to come up with the full $1.8 million and I was off and running. I opened up six stores throughout New York's Long Island and Westchester counties, did it all in the space of 17 months and started racking up big earnings. Although the Manhasset store proved to be a loser, the others generated roughly $600,000 each, on an annual basis. So my store sales were about $3.2 million, wholesale ice cream sales were good for another $2 million and my bottom line, after subtracting loan repayments, was approximately $1 million.''

Two of the biggest growth capital companies are:

1. Commercial Credit Capital Corp.—800-638-0660
2. Aetna Business Credit—800-334-3061

A LITTLE KNOWN AREA OF BANKING

• **Investment Banks.** When you are looking for the big money sources—the kinds of financing that can make a small business big—there is one type of outfit that can put you in touch with all the powers that be. For, behind the national network of main street bankers doing business in thousands of local branches, there is another layer of American banks that few ever see or hear about. It is the quiet, conservative and complex world of investment banking. Here, without checking accounts, savings plans or credit cards, most of the biggest financing deals are planned and implemented. Investment banks do not serve consumers: they are specialists in the needs of commerce and industry. Although they are often associated with the huge corporations of the Fortune 500, most serve a wide range of clients. Investment banks can, in fact, be of immense value to small companies (mostly leveraged entrepreneurs) by helping them secure extraordinary amounts of long-term financing. This is the ''free enterprise private loan pipeline'' in its most classic form.

In this type of relationship, the client pays the investment bankers an annual retainer in exchange for a set schedule of services. Although the fee is steep (in the $25,000 to $50,000 a year range), companies committed to long-term growth will likely find it a worthy investment. Investment bankers can help the company establish credibility with the most lucrative loan sources.

Owner-managers may also work with investment bankers on a project basis. When a company's growth pains call for heavy doses of capital, management simply calls on the investment bank to help raise the funds. Investment bankers generally use any of the following procedures:

• Arrange "private placement" loans with pension funds or insurance companies. For small companies, the amounts available range up to about $10 million, interest rates hover a few points above prime and terms extend out to 15 years.

• Take the company public. If rapid growth through public ownership appears to be the best approach, the bank will arrange a sale of stock or bonds in the public markets. This is a complex procedure, involving substantial fees and paperwork. Investment bankers generally charge eight to ten percent of the capital raised this way (compared to about a two percent fee for "private placements").

Investment banks are best at delivering the financial support emerging firms need to move out of the minor leagues. Bank executives have the clout, the know-how and the muscle to raise large sums of expansion capital.

"Every small company must cross a number of critical thresholds as it moves up the growth ladder," says Josiah Low, a managing director of Merrill Lynch—White Weld Capital Markets Group, a national investment banking outfit. "Typically, the firm goes from tiny entrepreneurship, to $1 million in revenues and then to $10 million and up. Once the company gets into the $1 to $10 million range, it becomes too big and complicated for the owner to do everything himself. He needs help in controlling the venture and keeping it pointed in the right direction."

That's where investment bankers come in. Promising small companies can pass through each threshold by bringing financial experts into the picture at an early stage. Working closely with the entrepreneurs, investment bankers keep tabs on the company's progress, advise when to seek additional capital and work with the client to get the needed funding.

• Help clients prepare the comprehensive "business plans" many lenders require before authorizing major loans. "Business plans" include professional cash flow analyses, balance sheets, income statements, market survey and management biographies. Many investment bankers go with their clients to present these plans to the Small Business Administration, commercial banks and business credit companies.

"Our flexibility is the key to our effectiveness," says Tony La Croix, vice president of Advest, Inc., a brokerage and investment banking outfit. "We often tap several different sources to arrange a single financing. Different investors fit into different risk categories—and we use them all. We might use a government loan, a private placement and equity funding all in the same deal. The objective is to get the client the needed money."

For big-thinking entrepreneurs, investment bankers can prove to be ideal partners in the business building process. They can add the element of financial sophistication most small companies lack, but desperately need in the search for major financing. Accountants, attorneys and trade associations can recommend established investment bankers.

USING TRADE CREDIT

Certain types of financing are what we call "secondary sources." Establishing trade credit is one of them. But remember, as a leveraged entrepreneur, you want to track down and utilize every possible source of outside financing. Every way to make borrowed money work for you fits into your master plan.

Establishing good trade credit is one way to get goods and services moving through a small firm without putting cash up front. Companies prepared to demonstrate some indication to repay can often obtain 30 to 90 days of interest-free credit from suppliers. And this absence of interest charges means you can avoid one of the real burdens of traditional financing. The trick to successful use of trade credit is to obtain inventories from suppliers, sell the goods and collect on the sales before payments are due and then pay the supplier with the receipts. Work out all trade credit plans by discussing your business needs with suppliers. Remember, the trick here is to be tough—to deal from a position of strength and to drive a hard bargain. Suppliers will not volunteer credit but will often provide it if you make clear that it is a prerequisite to doing business with them.

Just like many other financing opportunities, this one goes to the entrepreneurs with the guts and the know-how to seize it—to demand it.

"Luck was with me when I opened my auto supply shop at the busy corner of Central Ave and Barton Street," says Keith L. of Chicago, Ill. "Of course, I'd like to say that it is my skills as a merchant that made my store the biggest grosser of its kind in the city, but I think location had more to do with it than anything else. In just three short years, I'm doing better than $5 million a year—in parts, tires and repairs.

"Anyway, all of the tire companies shadow me like they're my twin brothers—begging to sell me more, to be exclusive dealers, you know how it is. Well, I finally got wise and decided to parlay my clout into hard cash. I made an exclusive deal with one of the tire outfits but they had to pay dearly for it. I get so much trade credit from them that all the risk in tire selling is now on their shoulders not mine. I stock all that I want, boast a huge inventory and have none of the usual inventory fears because none of my money is tied up in it. They take the risk and I have the cash for other purposes—like expanding to another shop in a nearby town."

Entrepreneurs in the know can search around for outfits specializing in "leveraged lease" arrangements. This often results in the lowest possible rates to the lessee. With leveraged leasing, the lessor uses some aspect of the tax structure to gain added tax advantages—and then passes on these advantages to the lessee in the form of lower rates. Let's say a deal is for equipment costing $50,000. Using a leveraged lease, the lessor may put up $10,000 and finance the rest with a non-recourse loan. This means the lessor gets the full tax advantage of a $50,000 purchase even though the actual investment is only $10,000. These leveraged benefits can be used to offer highly-attractive benefits to the lessee, or the techniques of leveraged leasing can be used by the lessee to take full advantage of the tax breaks.

Remember, the strategy of leveraged finance emphasizes not only the acquisition of borrowed funds but also the optimum use of those funds for business growth and expansion. By using leasing to acquire some business assets, you can pay for them from current earnings rather than shelling out lump sums of precious capital. Through leasing, someone else is financing your equipment—be it cars, trucks, machines, furniture, computers, copiers, or office buildings.

SALE AND LEASEBACK DEALS

Lenders reluctant to make traditional loans may be ready and willing to offer small companies "sale and leaseback" deals. Under this arrangement, the firm sells the bank or finance company any previously-owned equipment or facilities for 100 percent of the current market value—and then leases back the assets with regular payments. Cash from this sale of assets can be used by you for pressing business needs, expansion plans and the like.

LEASING—ACQUIRING BUSINESS ASSETS WITHOUT CASH

Somewhat related to sale and leaseback arrangements, the overall process of business leasing itself can aid leveraged entrepreneurs by helping you acquire business assets without paying cash up front. This increasingly popular option to traditional ownership reduces the need for huge capital outlays, offers added flexibility and provides some substantial service benefits. Considering the importance of utilizing costly, sophisticated equipment these days, leasing's advantages may be crucial. "The climate has never been more favorable for smaller companies to consider leasing," says the president of a major lease consulting firm. "Rates are relatively low and lease deals can be arranged for virtually every type of equipment and facility. There is so much competition among lessors, in fact, that companies considering leasing can virtually write their own ticket. They can hold out for both extremely low rates as well as the best possible terms. It's really a lessee's market."

Experts recommend that owner-managers inexperienced in the complexities of lease financing turn to competitive bidding to draw out the best available lease terms. This is done by simply contacting five or more leasing companies, submitting equipment specifications and requesting the most favorable lease quotes. Names of reputable lessors can be found in the yellow pages, in business service directories or through trade associations.

Small business owners interested in further exploring the pros and cons of leasing should bear in mind the following pointers:

• A recent ruling of the National Accounting Standards Board requires that all lease transactions be reported on a company's balance sheet. This means that lease liabilities will now be evident to potential creditors.

• Lease financing may be available when all other sources of credit are closed. The intense competition in the business equipment leasing industry is prompting some firms to accept less than ideal credit ratings. This may be a foot in the door for newly-launched or hard-pressed small companies that are unable to get bank financing.

• Small companies with leased equipment can trade in these assets for newer models at the end of the lease period. This reduces the risk of winding up with obsolete equipment and eliminates the need to sell off older units.

• In return for a set fee, lease consultants or accountants can determine—through the "discounted cash flow" formula—which mode of equipment financing is best for a specific company's financial position. The computation compares the relative merits of leasing, bank financing and outright purchases.

• Lease deals are generally based on fixed rates while other types of financing, including bank loans, may be tied to floating rates. Floating rates move up or down according to market conditions and are therefore relatively unpredictable.

As we see, the free enterprise financing pipeline is rich and diverse. It is important for you, as a leveraged entrepreneur, to explore each and every source available to you. The next chapter focuses on even more extraordinary ways of raising money to start or expand your business.

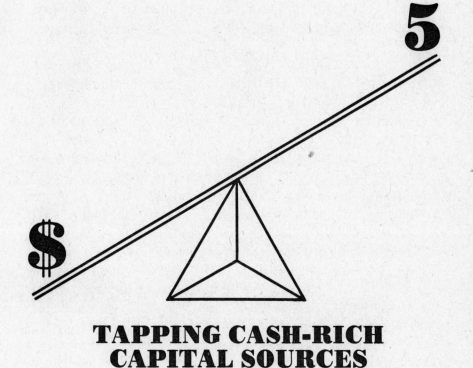

TAPPING CASH-RICH CAPITAL SOURCES

There are avenues of free enterprise financing that you will probably want to approach only after achieving success in the first stages of business growth. These tend to be the Daddy Warbucks of the leveraging strategy, the sources of really big money. Although some of the financing sources explored in previous chapters also qualify for the big leagues—and thus can provide very large amounts of capital—we have reserved this section for sources that we consider to be unusually rewarding to the leveraged financier.

You will notice immediately that unlike the previous sources discussed, most of these are not loans. By and large they involve a trade-off: giving up a share or piece of the business in return for investment capital. This is what is commonly referred to as equity capital. Some people confuse the terms borrowing and equity (or investment) capital. But there is a big difference. You do not have to repay equity capital as you would a loan. It's the money you get by selling a part interest in your business. In most cases, equity sources are interested in potential income rather than in an immediate return on their investment.

This willingness to rate an investment on the quality of its long-term potential, rather than the quick buck, is one reason why equity investors are often willing to accept levels of risk which are deemed far too great by traditional lenders. For the opportunity to multiply an investment ten or one hundred fold, many equity investors will gamble on the long shots. There have, in fact, been scores of cases where $100,000 or so invested returned $10 million or more; where $10 million invested parlayed itself into $70 million and up. Although these jackpots are few and far between, it is the memory of them that keeps equity capital flowing. Each investor wants to be the one to cash in on the next goldmine. It is your responsibility then to build an aura for your business that says, "Yes, big money can be made here." You must present your business to investors with such appeal and promise that they are willling to gamble on you. This persuasiveness—and the ability to present a professional business plan—are hallmarks of really successful leveraged entrepreneurs, of those who know how to attract capital to build their companies, while others assume most of the risks. Again, these persuasive and professional techniques will be discussed in later chapters. For now, let's examine some of these extraordinary capital sources.

VENTURE CAPITAL

A primary source of finance for new and expanding firms, venture capital is devoted almost exclusively to those businesses considered too risky by banks and other traditional lenders. For a share of the profits, venture capitalists take a chance on launching new firms which might otherwise never see the light of day. Although venture capital is not limited to this, it is best known for the support of high-technology companies.

The availability of venture capital funds fluctuates with the state of the economy. In past recessions, for example, venture capital has all but dried up. When this happens, the impact on entrepreneurs is swift and staggering: new technologies die on the vine, promising products never leave the drawing boards and thousands of good ideas never get off the ground for lack of capital. So in spite of all the benefits of venture capital as a source of high-risk funds, one must bear in mind that the chances for securing this money are best when the national economy is robust and investor confidence is strong. At these times, the faucets of venture capital are wide open. A good yardstick for all of this is the stock market: a strong bull market is the best catalyst for generating venture capital.

The Range of Venture Capital

Venture capitalists range from one-person operations to large departments of major commercial banks. Although the terms of financing vary depending on the type of venture and the risks involved, most demand a healthy percentage of the business in return. It is also a common practice for venture capitalists to provide intensive managerial as well as financial assistance.

"The important point for those seeking venture capital to remember," says a top executive with a California-based venture ourfit, "is that a professional presentation of their business concepts is vital. Venture capitalists are most likely to work with those managers best able to prove that their ventures will succeed."

The venture capital industry is more visible and organized than ever before in its history. There is now a National Venture Capital Association which is a forum or trade group for many of the independent venture capital outfits in the U.S. The industry has assets of more than $3 billion and invests between $500 and $600 million a year. Experts put the number of venture capital firms at between 400 and 500. According to the Guide to Venture Capital Sources, these firms are broken down into the following categories:

Private Venture Capital Firms: These are mostly professional partnerships and corporations that have been backed by institutional investors. The big money behind these operations comes from insurance companies, pension funds and the like.

Family Venture Capital Firms: A good number of the nation's super-rich families have traditionally channelled a percentage of their funds to high-risk venture opportunities. Some of the best-known names in the land have engaged in this and have invested many millions in everything from scientific products to resorts.

Small Business Investment Companies: About half of the nation's SBICs (discussed in Chapter III) are active primarily in venture activities; the others prefer to do secured lending rather than equity funding.

Venture Capital Divisions of Large Corporations: Here, divisions or subsidiaries of well-known corporate giants make investments in what they believe are promising products, companies, technologies or industries. One good example is the Exxon Corporation which has invested heavily in, among other things, small firms developing word processing systems and facsimile transmission devices. This type of venture outfit can be a source of substantial funds.

Investment Bankers: As I mentioned earlier, behind the national network of commercial and savings banks, there is another world of banking that serves businesses exclusively. This is the world of investment banking. These financial institutions specialize in helping companies raise money through loan and equity sources. Some investment banks invest their own funds in venture capital deals; others can help to arrange for this financing.

Which type of venture capital source would be best for your needs? Which would be most likely to come up with the needed money to leverage your business? Again, according to The Guide To Venture Capital Sources, family-run venture outfits are usually interested in newly-launched firms or those still on the drawing boards rather than in companies seeking expansion. Also, they prefer business ideas that will have a powerful and positive effect on improving social conditions. The private venture capital firms, which range in size from approximately $2 million to $80 million, have widely-divergent investment criteria. Some prefer to invest in start-up situations, which are the riskiest of all and are therefore the hardest to attract capital for; others specialize in second- and third-stage financing, which really means providing growth money for expanding companies.

The large corporations with venture capital operations are often most interested in seeding new firms, helping them develop and mature and then acquiring them as divisions or subsidiaries. For many leveraged entrepreneurs this can be the best of both worlds: a major corporation funds the venture in its earliest days, assumes the greatest risk and then buys it out when and if success is achieved.

It is safe to say that no more than 20 percent of the nation's venture capital firms are active in business start-ups. Start-up situations are those companies that are still in the process of being formed or that have been in business for less than a year and have not yet accepted orders. It is at the first stage of development and after that the majority of venture firms like to get involved. First-stage financing, for example, is for companies that have already used their seed capital to manufacture a product prototype or to get themselves started in some other way. Many venture capitalists prefer to enter the scene at this stage because the company they will invest in can show some tangible evidence of growth potential (like a working prototype of the company's key product).

Leveraged entrepreneurs who do go on to achieve initial success may find that their company's growth curve demands tremendous amounts of capital and that this can only be satisfied by a public offering (to be discussed in this chapter). In cases such as these, venture capitalists can make so-called "bridge loans," which are designed for firms going public in from six months to a year from the date of the loan. "Bridge loans" are generally repaid from the capital generated through the public offering.

The amount of money that can be obtained from venture capitalists is virtually unlimited—certainly, multi-million dollar deals are quite common. What the venturers want for their investments are good prospects for steady growth over a given period of time. Most look for a profit of at least five times their stake within five years.

Keep in mind, however, that the venture capitalists requirements are only one side of the coin. You, too, must be happy with the relationship. This means making sure that you select an investor who stands to offer your business the most in terms of management support and financial backing. You should also feel comfortable working with the firm or individual.

One good measure here is to check out the venture capitalist's track record. Get the names of four or five companies the firm has invested in and worked with and see how the relationship has gone from the entrepreneur's point of view. Also, get a complete breakdown of the venturer's fee policies. Are there any hidden payments built into the deal. Some venture capital outfits require that closing costs, legal fees and investigation costs be paid by the firm seeking capital; other venturers absorb these expenses in their own account. What's more, find out if the venture capital firm's consulting services will be billed to you or be provided free of charge. This distinction can mean thousands of dollars.

As we have noted, venture capitalists invest in your business in return for a stake in the enterprise. Their capital is not a loan—it is an equity investment. The types of financial instruments used to finance venture investments vary with the capitalist's policies, the kind of venture he's investing in and the amount of risk involved. The following are the major instruments for venture investments:

Common Stock. This stock is used most often for buying part ownership of a company. Common stock pays dividends and grants the holder the right to share in certain corporate decisions. The drawback here, however, is that if the firm goes broke, these stockholders have the last claim on its assets.

Convertible Preferred Stock. This stock gives added rights to the investor (compared to common stockholders). There is greater opportunity to influence control of the company and to obtain liquidity.

Subordinated Debt. This alternative to the equity approach is used in those instances where the investor prefers the security of a debt instrument and the company does not want to hamper its ability to borrow from banks or other sources. If this subordinated debt does not dominate the firm's capital structure, then senior lenders will consider it to be equity. In most cases, this means you'll be able to get more money from lending sources in addition to the venture capital source.

HOW VENTURE CAPITAL HELPED
BARNEY L. COMBINE TWO
CAREERS TO START HIS FORTUNE

Barney L. of San Antonio, Texas is a perfect example of a leveraged entrepreneur who has made exceptional use of venture capital funds. A jack-of-all trades for the first twenty years of his working life, Barney kicked around the country as a writer, editor and, of all things, a building contractor. Born into a family construction business, Barney learned how to put up houses before he left high school. It was his father's dream that he come and join the firm and then take it over in the future, but Barney would have none of that. All the years he spent learning to hammer together two by fours, he was dreaming of his first love: writing. From earliest childhood, he had a way with words, and although his old man tried to discourage it, Barney always knew that he'd have to at least try to make a career as a writer.

Landing a job with a Dallas-based photo magazine, Barney wrote about Texas business and soon found he was being recognized as somewhat of an expert in the field. His work won a national journalism award and that was enough to prompt a call from the **Wall Street Journal** inviting Barney to join the paper's staff. It was the break he was waiting for and he flew the world over, covering stories on a great variety of business trends and events. Gradually, however, his expertise in construction became evident to the **Journal**'s managing editor and Barney was asked to specialize in that part of the news.

As often happens, Barney's success in his chosen field led him to dream of another challenge. He started missing his work in the family firm, clearing huge plots of virgin land and watching a development rise where once there was nothing. So, leaving his writing behind, Barney headed back to Texas, to stand by his father's side, sharpen his knowledge of the financial end of the business, and gradually to serve as the ramrod of the family venture.

"I was actually torn between both careers—writing and building," Barney explains. "It's strange, I know, but it's true. I was really going through personal hell trying to figure out what to do when it hit me: why not combine both types of work. I realized that there was a crying need for a new type of construction industry publication—a magazine with international appeal that would cover the field for builders, architects and even real estate agents."

Barney flew to New York and brought his idea to a friend he'd made while working for the **Journal**. Arlen K., a former Time, Inc. executive, knew the magazine industry inside and out and was an ideal person to consult with. After a bit of research into the construction magazine field, Arlen believed the idea was an all-out winner. The potential subscriber market was there and the advertising bucks were ready and waiting.

Putting it all on paper in a formal cash-flow projection, Barney and Arlen (who had decided to form a corporation, Bar-len Publishing) were astounded themselves to see that they had an earnings potential of $6 million after only three years. And that was only the start. It looked as though Barney, who was born to a comfortable family running a moderately successful business ($2.5 million annually) could get really rich for the first time in his life. He wanted it badly—not just for the things it could buy, but also to "prove to dad that I could make it through the field I had chosen—and make it even bigger than him."

The one stumbling block for Bar-len Publishing was the need for substantial amounts of capital. Just to put together a small prototype issue of the magazine, which would be used to interest advertisers to take advance pages, had a lofty price tag of $75,000. Together, the partners had only about $30,000 but they were fortunate enough to touch bases at this time with a mutual friend who happened to be looking for some promising investments. More than just lend the needed $45,000, the outside investor explained the basics of leveraged finance to the two would-be publishing tycoons and made them recognize that they could borrow their way to success. He was willing to be the first money source. In return, he wanted three percent of the magazine's earnings over the first ten years. If there were no earnings, the debt would be cancelled; if the venture scored big, he could multiply his $45,000 many times over.

Now sufficiently funded to publish their prototype edition, Barney and Arlen went to work producing a sophisticated and attractively-designed magazine. To save money, Barney developed most of the stories and did the writing himself. The prototype was printed in four-color on glossy stock and an accompanying advertising rate card was produced. Armed with demographic studies of potential readers—and with copies of the sample magazine—Arlen hit the streets of Madison Avenue trying to line up interested advertisers—those willing to commit to the publication before it was a proven commodity. To encourage their cooperation, Bar-len established charter ad rates for those advertisers willing to take a chance—and those rates would be guaranteed for the first year regardless of how big circulation became. This was a powerful inducement: advertisers could buy space for perhaps 25 percent of the going rate if they took a chance, many became charter supporters and the publication proved to be successful.

Bar-len needed commitments for 35 ad pages to start work on producing a full-scale magazine and to develop the all-important subscriber base. They got 72 pages—enough to make the periodical an in-the-black success with the very first issue. That is an awesome feat in the always tough and competitive publishing world.

Now that the potential rewards were skyrocketing, so too were the financial requirements. The initial $75,000 kitty was more than depleted (leaving a $7000 debt) in producing the prototype issue and in sales expenses (Arlen's sales efforts to potential advertisers were costly in terms of lavish lunches, dinners, etc). What's more, the expense so far was only peanuts—just enough to give the advertising community a look at this new property. To develop a circulation base, hire a staff, rent adequate offices, advertise and promote and print the publication for one year alone, Bar-len now needed $2.4 million.

"We did a good deal of searching around for the money—went through the traditional bank and government routes—and found that there was a good deal of resistance to coming up with the kind of money we needed. Most traditional lenders didn't feel comfortable with publishing ventures, didn't think we had enough to go on to feel confident of our success and told us we were asking for too much money. What we started hearing from a number of experts is that we should turn to venture capitalists."

And that's just what they did. Although Barney and Arlen did not relish the idea of sharing control or ownership with outside investors, they needed lots of money and, as Arlen put it, "beggars can't be choosy. And hell, if we could make $6 million, so what if we had to share some of it. After all, they were putting up the money, they were taking the risk."

KEY REFERENCES

To find the ideal venture capital firm to work with, Bar-len used an approach which is acceptable for a wide range of entrepreneurs. Simply buy or borrow one of the reference books listing venture capital sources and providing the following information for each:

- Name
- Address
- Names of Top Officers
- Telephone Numbers
- The Type Of Venture Capital Source It Is
- Its Affiliations (Banks, etc)
- The Types Of Projects It Prefers To Finance
- The Types Of Financing It Does
- The Industries It Prefers To Work In
- Its Geographical Preferences (If Any)
- Its Methods Of Compensation
- How Long It Has Been In Business
- The Size Of Its Minimum Investments
- The Size Investments It Prefers To Make
- The Number Of Deals It Has Completed In The Past Year
- The Amount Of Money It Has Invested In The Past Year

Some sample listings from such publications are as follows:

BLYTH EASTMAN DILLON & CO.,
 INCORPORATED

555 California Street
San Francisco, CA 94104
415-382-800

Officer

William K. Bowles, Jr., Sr. V.P.

Type of company

Private venture firm investing own
 capital
Investment banking firm investing funds
 of partners and clients
Investment banking firm evaluating and
 analyzing venture projects and arranging private placements

Affiliation
INA Corp., insurance company

Project preferences/
Type of financing
Start-up financing
First-stage financing
Second-stage financing
Third-stage financing
Buy-out or acquisition financing

Minimum operating data
Annual Sales—nominal
P & L—losses (profits projected after 2
years)

Industry preferences
None

Geographical preferences
Near major metropolitan area

Methods of compensation
Professional fee if deal closes

Additional information about
company
Years in business—over 5
Minimum investment—$100-300,000
Preferred investment—$600,000 and
over
Will function in either active or passive
role
Deals completed in past year—2-5
Invested during past year—$1 million or
less

BRENTWOOD ASSOCIATES

11661 San Vincente Boulevard Rm. 707
Los Angeles, CA 90049
213-826-6581

Partners
Frederick J. Warren, Gen. Ptnr.
B. K. Hagopian, Gen. Ptnr.
Timothy M. Pennington, Gen. Ptnr.
Roger Davisson

Whom to contact
Any of above

Type of investor
Private venture firm investing own
capital

Affiliation
Has wholly owned SBIC subsidiary

Project preferences/
Type of financing
First-stage financing
Buy-out or acquisition financing

Minimum operating data
Annual sales—nominal
P & L—losses (profits projected in 3
years)

Industry preferences
• **Technology**
Integrated circuitry, materials
Optics technology
Pollution control
Data processing
Graphic arts
Communications
• **Computer related**
Peripheral equipment
Data communications
Word processing
• **Manufacturing**
Various types
• **Medical**
Clinical laboratories
Drugs and medicines
Medical instruments
• **Natural resources**
Oil and gas
Specialty raw materials
• **Retail**
Mail order
• **Services**
Advertising
CATV
Specialty consulting

Geographical preferences

None

Methods of compensation

Return on investment is most important but also charge legal expenses and out-of-pocket expenses

Addition information about company

Years in business—3-5
Minimum investment—$100-300,000
Preferred investment—$300-600,000
Prefer active role as a deal originator
Deals completed in past year—over 5
Invested during past year—$1-5 million

NEILL H. BROWNSTEIN

63000 Sand Hill Road
Menlo Park, CA 94025
415-854-2606

Whom to contact

Sol Miller

BRYAN & EDWARDS

235 Montgomery Street Rm 2220
San Francisco, CA 94104
415-421-9990

Partners

John M. Bryan, Gen. Ptnr.
Wm. C. Edwards, Gen. Ptnr.
Alan Brudos

Whom to contact

Any of above

Type of investor

Private venture firm investing own capital

Affiliation

Two SBICs are also operated from this office. Edvestco Inc. and Bryan Capital Inc.

Project preferences/
Type of financing

First-stage financing
Second-stage financing
Third-stage financing
Buy-out or acquisition financing

Minimum operating data

No specific requirement

Industry preferences

None

Geographical preferences

West Coast

Methods of compensation

Return on investment is primary concern; no fees

Additional information about company

Years in business—over 5
Minimum investment—$100,000 or less
Preferred investment—$50-250,000
Will function in either active or passive role
Deals completed in past year—2-5
Invested during past year—$1 million or less

Although commercial and investment bankers can also be good sources of information on venture capitalists, use of these books give you reference works for the many hundreds of venture firms operating in the nation. By reading through the listings, you, as an entrepreneur, can isolate those venture capital outfits which are most likely to do business with you: those interested in making the right-size investments in your particular industry. The best procedure is to isolate five or six of the venturers who seem to offer the best hope for financing and then make appointments to see them.

"That's exactly what we did," says Arlen, who, along with Barney, met with three venture capital firms before coming to an agreement with one. "We were prepared to travel aross the country to meet with the best firms, but that proved to be unnecessary. It just so happens that we made a deal with the venture arm of a big New York brokerage house. They were willing to come up with all of the money needed in return for a 45 percent interest in our company."

The jury is still out on Bar-len's magazine. Production delays hampered the start of the publication and foul-ups with a computer facility stalled the subscription mailings. There were 60,000 subscribers signed up before the troubles began, however, and the editors felt confident that the magazine would fill a real void in the marketplace. Madison Avenue also continues to be enthusiastic.

So, although we do not know if there is another **Business Week** in the making here, we have been shown the power of leveraged finance through venture capital. If the magazine is a good product, success will come to it in time. What's more important from your standpoint is that two entrepreneurs started with only $30,000 and used the free enterprise system to get more than $2.5 million for the purpose of making a business dream come true.

GOING PUBLIC

In many cases, venture capitalists are willing to risk substantial amounts of money in the hope that the firm they invest in will eventually go public. Then, all shareholders can have a way of gauging the real market value of their holdings and can enjoy a good measure of liquidity.

Going public is, in fact, the way the greatest amount of business capital is generally raised. Many small firms, at some time in their existence, ponder the prospect of going public—but few really know how it works and what it entails. Put simply, going public refers to the sale of a company's securities to a relatively large number of people.

Although most any size firm may go public, the process is not as simple as putting up products or services for sale. An offering of corporate stock is one phase of a rather lengthy and complex legal process, carefully controlled and regulated by the Securities and Exchange Commission. The SEC, empowered to enforce federal securities legislation, maintains supervision over the nation's public companies.

The increased supervision over the company's operations is a major factor to be weighed by the owner-manager considering a public offering. For many managers, it is an intolerable interference with a personal, and somewhat private, style of doing business. Public ownership requires the regular disclosure of financial and operating information to the commission and to the firm's stockholders. Another major drawback to public ownership (similarly with certain venture capital deals) emerges when the offering is for more than 50 percent of the company's stock. This, of course, makes you vulnerable to outside control.

There are, however, great advantages to going public. The first, and most important from our standpoint, is the accumulation of additional capital. A stock offering enables your firm to raise money for expansion, improvements and other operating needs. The second advantage is that the market mechanism attaches a general value to your firm's securities and enables you to determine the worth of personal holdings. What's more, since masses of people can be drawn into an offering, wide excitement about a new business, product, invention or industry can be translated into huge amounts of capital. If your business is attractive—and the offering is professionally handled—investors may wait in line to invest with you. It has happened many times.

A change in the regulations has recently made it simpler for small companies to go public. The easier and simpler Regulation A procedure can now be used to raise up to $1.5 million (the cut off point for Regulation A filings used to be $500,000). Regulation A filings are simplified registrations that can be processed through an SEC regional office. This requires less legal preparation, and less cost, than a standard offering.

A stock offering to raise more than $1.5 million, however, must be filed through the SEC headquarters in Washington, D.C. Management must submit a registration statement to the commission. The statement is a legal document containing a prospective on the securities offering. It is a report of vital information, including a description of the company and the stock being offered, the name of the underwriter, names and experience of top company officers and directors, salaries of executive management, articles of incorporation and the company's by-laws.

The completed statement is forwarded to the SEC with a fee based on the value of the offering. Examiners at the commission study the statement to verify conformity with all legal requirements. If changes must be made, a letter of comment is issued to the company's management.

Management may simply comply with the new directions or seek a conference with commission officials. Management then files an amendment to the registration statement. If the amended statement complies with all SEC requirements, a mutually-agreeable date is set for the statement to be "declared effective" and the issue may be sold. The company is then a public firm. It must retain the advice of a knowledgeable attorney, report to the SEC, cater to stockholders and operate in a more open manner than ever before. But there is also a good chance that it will have more capital than the founder ever dreamed possible.

The success of public offerings is very dependent on the mood of the stock market: bull markets generate the kind of confidence in people that bode well for public offerings; bear markets have just the opposite effect. In times of recession, in fact, when the market has performed miserably, public issues have all but dried up. So the temper of the times is a very important consideration in your deliberations of when and if to go public.

Bear in mind that you can not start a company today and take it public tomorrow. The securities laws are designed to protect the public from schemes designed simply to make the corporation rich. An SEC requirement is that you must have at least three years of audited financial data available for its examination. Also, if you are seeking more than the Regulation A offering allows, the process of going public is complex and costly. It can wind up costing your firm $100,000 or more.

Probably the first step in going public is to select a competent investment bank or underwriter to handle the transaction. This institution can, in fact, be consulted even before you make the final decision to go ahead with the offering. Investment bankers are trained to analyze all of the facts about your company, the current state of the market and the levels of investor confidence. They can be a reliable source of information on whether or not going public is the correct route for your company. Again, consult a good directory of investment bankers specializing in small company issues. These publications list vital information about investment banking houses and give examples of the issues they have underwritten including the name of the company, description of the business, date of the underwriting, amount of the underwriting, amount of the underwriter's fee, price of the issue and the earnings per share in a recent year.

Here is an example of a listing. The bold face names in capital letters are those of the investment bankers; the companies written below that are issues that have been underwritten by the bankers:

BATEMAN, EICHLER, HILL, RICHARDS, INC.

460 South Spring Street
Los Angeles, CA 90013
213-625-3545

Willard G. De Groot, Chm. & Chief
  Exec.

Executives Industries
Motor homes and recreational vechicles
Apr. 1976
$6,100,000 underwritten
$396,000 fee
$20.357 per share
$1.10 earnings per share last year

SBE Inc.
Citizens band radios
Jan. 1976
$5,500,000 underwritten
$11.00 per share
$1.60 earnings per share last year

WD-40 Co.
Multiple use petroleum product
Dec. 1972
$4,950,000 underwritten

$420,000 fee plus warrants
$16.50 per share
$.73 earnings per share last year

Drewry Photocolor Corp.
Photographic processing
Nov. 1972
$2,400,000 underwritten
$204,000 fee
$10.00 per share
$.77 earnings per share last year

Macrodata Corp.
Semiconductor testing equipment
Oct. 1972
$3,720,000 underwritten
$316,200 fee plus warrants
$12.00 per share
$.32 earnings per share last year

Computer Election Systems, Inc.
Punch card voting equipment
July 1972
$3,906,000 underwritten
$332,010 fee plus warrants
$12.00 per share
$.54 earnings per share last year

Vagabond Motor Hotels, Inc.
Motor hotels
May 1972
$4,725,000 underwritten
$370,000 fee
$15.75 per share
$.58 earnings per share last year

General Automation, Inc.
Manufactures minicomputers
Jan. 1972
$3,600,000 underwritten; $285,000 fee
$18.00 per share
$.00 earnings per share last year

Executive Industries, Inc.
Manufactures motor homes
Dec. 1971
$2,250,000 underwritten
$201,250 fee plus warrants
$10.00 per share
$.58 earnings per share last year

BEAR, STEARNS & CO.

55 Water Street
New York, NY 10041
212-952-5000

Salim L. Lewis, Ptnr.

Safetran Systems Corp.
Electrical and mechanical equipment for
   the railroad industry
Dec. 1971
$3,000,000 underwritten
$260,000 fee
$7.50 per share
$1.15 earnings per share last year

BIRR, WILSON & CO., INC.

155 Sansome Street
San Francisco, CA 94104
415-983-7700

John W. Jalonen, Chm.
H. Theodore Birr III, Pres.
Theodore M. Wight, Corp. Finance
   Dept.

Showboat, Inc.
Gambling casino/hotel
Sept. 1972
$1,750,000 underwritten
$164,000 fee
$17.50 per share
$1.64 earnings per share last year

Under Sea Industries, Inc.
Aquatic Sport diving equipment
Sept. 1972
$2,550,000 underwritten
$204,000 fee plus warrants
$12.75 per share
$.48 earnings per share last year

Advanced Chemical Technology
Plastics and plastics related products
July 1972
$4,180,000 underwritten
$354,850 fee plus warrants
$11.00 per share
$.46 earnings per share last year

Microform Data Systems, Inc.
Information retrieval systems
Apr. 1972
$2,273,750 underwritten
$214,638 fee plus warrants
$4.25 per share
Loss—last year's report

Pacific Northwest Development Corp.
Real estate development
Mar. 1972
$1,999,998 underwritten
$342,222 fee plus warrants
$9.00 per share
$.74 earnings per share last year

Sigmaform Corp.

Plastic cable tubing
Mar. 1972
$1,927,170 underwritten
$188,445 fee plus warrants
$9.00 per share
$.10 earnings per share last year

Lindal Cedar Homes, Inc.

Manufacturers precut cedar homes
Nov. 1971
$3,000,000 underwritten
$255,000 fee plus warrants
$15.00 per share
$.53 earnings per share last year

BLACK & CO., INC.

American Bank Building
Portland, OR 97205
503-248-9600

Lawrence S. Black, Pres.

Gregg's Food Products, Inc.

Various food products
Apr. 1972
$2,975,000 underwritten
$255,000 fee
$7.00 per share
$.38 earnings per share last year

D. H. BLAIR SECURITIES CORP.

437 Madison Avenue
New York, NY 10022
212-421-7030
Division of D. H. Blair & Co., Inc.

J. Morton Davis, Pres.

Digital Paging Systems, Inc.

Automated nationwide radio paging
  service
Apr. 1972
$3,300,000 underwritten
$360,000 fee
$11.00 per share

Leonard Silver International, Inc.

Wholesale distributor of giftware
Feb. 1972
$1,395,000 underwritten
$150,550 fee plus warrants
$9.00 per share
$.65 earnings per share last year

Danker & Wohlk, Inc.

Contact lenses
Dec. 1971
$1,050,000 underwritten
$130,000 fee plus warrants
$8.75 per share; including warrant to
  purchase a share at $8.75, initially;
  no previous market
$.20 earnings per share last year

Let's look at the case of a small business that has gone public and has done so successfully. In 1970, an investment banking house active in small issues took a venture position in an emerging electronics firm that we'll call Futura Energy Systems (FES). The outfit fared well, developed a small line of products which gained market acceptance and showed steady increases in sales and earnings. By 1975, the firm recorded revenues of about $12 million with an after-tax bottom line of slightly more than $1 million. It was at this time that the management of FES and the investment bankers started giving serious thought to taking the firm public: substantial capital was needed to build a foundation for significant future growth.

After careful analysis of FES' growth prospects, management and the bankers agreed that going public was advisable. Since a substantial amount of money was sought, the formal S1 registration statement (rather than the simplified Regulation A) was prepared by the company's attorneys and was reviewed by the underwriter. The underwriter arranged a "syndicate" of investment bankers to sponsor the issue across the nation (this is common practice) and FES management spent one month traveling from city to city to meet the bankers, hold "informational meetings," and answer questions about their company.

When the company did go public, in the spring of 1976, its stock was priced at $8 per share (this price is based on the company's earnings, the potential growth rate of the business and the price/earnings ratio of other public companies in similar industries). All 800,000 shares sold out almost immediately, yielding $6.4 million. From this, eight percent of the offering price (eight percent of $8 per share) was deducted for underwriting discounts and selling commissions. In addition, FES paid all of the expenses of the underwriting, which total almost $190,000. Subtracting these expenses and commissions, FES cleared about $5.7 million—a tidy haul.

It must be remembered, however, that this successful outcome is not always achieved. In many cases, the corporate offering is met with resistance or indifference on the part of the public. The stock does not sell and the company is left holding the bag for expenses of several hundred thousand dollars. What we are saying is that going public can be the best way to raise tremendous amounts of capital, but there are no guarantees.

Some of the failures in public offerings could be avoided by doing more work to encourage investor interest. Most small firms do not recognize the importance of investor relations and management does not know how to conduct this vital function. As we have noted, going public can be a complex, time-consuming process. Once the work has been accomplished, management tends to settle back and relax, assuming that magic will take over. This, of course, is a false assumption and is a prime cause for disappointment. Actually, going public is only half the effort. Management must then concentrate on developing ties with the financial community. This is especially true for the small company, because it does not command a natural audience like a General Motors or Westinghouse.

DEALING WITH FINANCIAL ANALYSTS

Management can best reach the investment community through financial analysts, who study public firms and issue research reports. Because the reports form the basis for the majority of investment decisions, they are well read and widely circulated. This helps the small firm replace investor apathy with considerable interest, and can bolster the stock, help raise additional capital and attract top-notch management personnel.

Management's first step is to find the analysts specializing in the firm's industry. Analysts are usually confined to a limited area of interest and the specialists names and affiliations may be found in the annual roster of the Federation of Financial Analysts or by calling the various brokerage firms. Once the target group of analysts has been selected, it is best to invite them to a meeting. In a survey of the National Investor Relations Institute (a group of executives responsible for financial community relations), 82 percent of the respondents named luncheon formats as the ideal arrangement for these meetings. The luncheon should be informal and limited to a relatively small number, which helps to stimulate in-depth discussions on the company's present status and future prospects.

It is best to extend the initial invitations to analysts through a third party well known in financial circles. The vast majority of respondents in the survey indicated that this duty is normally left to a public relations representative or their investment banker. In either case, a personal follow up letter should be issued by top management, requesting the analysts' attendance and providing the necessary details of time, date and location. A final telephone call a few days in advance will serve as a reminder to help generate maximum participation. A good rule of thumb, however, is that only 50 percent of the invited will attend.

Once the meeting has been set, management must work to take the fullest advantage of the opportunity. All plans must be for-

malized well in advance and final arrangements triple-checked so
that the firm presents an efficient, well-organized image. There is no
time to waste and no margin for mistakes. The luncheon should be
completed within two hours, with no more than half an hour devoted
to management's speech or presentation. The idea is to be brief,
concise, informative and interesting. This means eliminating a
lengthy history of the firm and concentrating on operating features.
Financial information is best discussed in conjunction with annual
and interim reports.

It is common practice to end the luncheon with a question-and-
answer period. At least 15 minutes should be allotted to this segment,
perhaps more, if the level of interest remains high. In addition, the
company president should invite each analyst to meet with him
privately for further questions—a popular gesture with the many
analysts who prefer to consult on a one-to-one basis.

The leveraged entrepeneur must regard the first luncheon as only one step in developing effective analyst contacts. The competition
for the attention of analysts is never-ending and requires regular
mail correspondence, telephone calls and personal meetings.
Keeping the analysts up-to-date on the company's progress is the key
to developing excellent relations with the financial community. And
good relations here will help you make all of your journeys into the
capital markets successful ones. Few things are more important to a
leveraged entrepreneur.

MERGERS

Another way to raise large sums of capital, and in some cases to
provide for a continuous flow of capital, is to merge your business
with another company.

The recent spate of billion dollar business takeovers has Wall
Steet buzzing with rumors of the next major acquisition. Talk of corporate conquests is now the hot topic of conversation in the nation's
financial circles.

Although big business has dominated the merger news, there's
plenty of activity in the small businesses sector too. The wave of
"mergermania" is moving along a broad front, sweeping up com-

panies of all sizes in its wake. For many business owners, the trend is a positive development, offering opportunities for rapid growth, instant liquidity, substantial capital and management clout.

Put simply, a merger is the fusion of two distinct business entities into a single organization. In small business transactions, mergers are usually voluntary: one firm simply sells out to another for stock, cash or both.

"The number of small business mergers is now reaching record levels," says Marshall and Stevens, Inc., a merger valuation service. "For every merger that makes national news, there are 20 or 30 smaller ones that go unnoticed. Many owners are recognizing that mergers offer the ideal solution for a host of business problems."

By attracting a merger partner, owners of closely-held companies can sell their interests and "bail out," thus turning years of hard work into liquid assets. For other entrepreneurs, mergers offer a good chance to obtain the capital necessary to keep the business growing. This is the only way some small firms can attract growth capital.

The first step in any merger is to properly value the interests up for sale. Here is where the majority of small firms get started on the wrong foot.

All too many mergers are conducted on emotion rather than facts or reason. The price of a deal is arrived at in a high-stakes poker atmosphere with neither side having full knowledge of the facts. In these situations, bluffing is routine and emotion often rules in setting the sale price.

Merger experts contend that owner-managers are not qualified to appraise their own firms. Most often, they base selling prices on balance sheet statistics which are inaccurate or out-of-date. Common mistakes include undervaluing assets, computing nonexistent assets and failing to add in the value of intangibles like trademarks, royalties and patents.

Professional assistance in pre-merger appraisals is available from private valuation services. In return for a fee based on the complexity of the study, valuation experts conduct a comprehensive appraisal of the firm, indicating a true market value on which to base the sale or purchase price.

"Mergers still offer small business owners the best chance to sell their companies at a good price," says Victor Niederhoffer of

Neiderhoffer, Cross & Zeckhauser, Inc., a merger consulting outfit. "And the good news is that sellers are getting more and more of the purchase price in cash. Although there are no guarantees, owners can expect a settlement based on 10 times current earnings or three times book value."

Merger consultants arrange the marriage between buyer and seller. A report on the company up for sale is circulated to a network of potential buyers. When interest is expressed, face-to-face meetings are set up. The process can take months or years and fees for the service range from three to ten percent of the selling price.

Companies with the following characteristics are most likely to attract merger offers:

- Depth of management below the top executive.
- Major facilities including plants and offices are owned by the company.
- Plants and other facilities are modern and are in good condition.
- Sales and earnings are healthy and rising steadily.
- Markets for the company's products and services are strong and growing.

Remember, you can hold out for mergers that suit your needs and that are designed to satisfy your particular requirements. One of the best ways to get tremendous amounts of growth capital is to seek a merger with a big corporation. The big firm will then use its cash, resources and skills to expand what was formerly your venture. Although you will lose sole ownership, you can retain shares in the merged corporation and you can keep your position as head of the company (although it will now be a part of the combined corporations). To explore the pros and cons of a merger, ask your banker or attorney for the name of a merger consultant. These outfits will look into the possibilities with you.

SILENT PARTNERS

One form of business financing that should not be overlooked or ignored is the good old silent partner. Yes, Virginia, there are investors out there in our diverse free enterprise system who have tons of cash and who are constantly on the prowl for lucrative investment opportunities. Some want to lend money as debt instruments; others want a piece of the business. Some stay away from start-up situations; others like nothing better than to take a flyer on an untested idea. Some limit their involvement to under $100,000; others like the high stakes games of $1 million or more.

The common thread which typifies silent partners is that they do not want to be involved in the day-to-day operations of your business. They are, as the term implies, "silent." In return for sound assurance that you will be able to reward their risk in you, most are content to keep quiet, watch from the sidelines and take their dividends as they come due. The beauty of working with silent partners is that it is all so simple: there are no SEC regulations, no stockholder meetings, no merger attorneys and no need to open your business operations to public scrutiny. You remain an independent entrepreneur in the purest form and yet have another person's money to use building your company.

The problem is, of course, that silent partners are not waiting on every street corner simply looking for places to invest their money. Most want to keep a low profile and once contacted, must be convinced that your venture is worthy of their risk. But because finding and convincing a silent partner can be well worth the effort, we certainly suggest this approach as one more way to harness the power of leveraged finance.

Where do you look for silent partners? The best place is under the Capital Available or Capital To Invest advertisements in the **Wall Street Journal**. Here, silent partners will often put out feelers for the kinds of deals they are interested in.

You can also generate interest on your own by taking out a Capital Wanted ad in the **Journal**. Other good sources are your banker, attorney and accountant. They may know of moneyed individuals willing to invest in your venture. And do not overlook your own circle of contacts including friends, business associates, relatives and doctors. Some of these people may be more than eager to invest with you. It certainly doesn't hurt to ask.

"I used to think that silent partners were only found in B movies," says Glen I. of Rochester, N.Y. "But when I started asking around, I found that they really do exist. And I'm not ashamed to say it—they've made me a rich man today."

A former employee of a tennis court building and management firm, Glen rose through the ranks to the vice presidency. Although he was pulling down $90,000 a year plus a company Mercedes, he wanted more—the sky's the limit opportunity of owning his own business.

"I needed capital—plenty of it—and someone told me that the best place to look for it was around my own country club. I started playing golf for the contacts I could make at it rather than for the sport." Glen's contacts turned out to be excellent. He started playing in a foursome that featured three doctors and himself. All were surgeons, well established and very wealthy.

"To top it all off, they were tennis nuts and wanted to be involved in the business. They were willing to exchange my knowledge of the business for cash—so they put up a total of $450,000. With that, we were able to get another $1 million of bank financing and I was on my own. I became president of GlenSports Tennis Unlimited, they continued to practice medicine and we all got richer than ever before."

GlenSports' first tennis facility proved to be an instant success and was soon duplicated with three additional centers and a squash facility. All are booked from morning to night, the pro shops alone gross close to $1 million annually and Glen's making more now in bonuses than he used to earn on salary.

"I'm rich now—getting richer all the time—and I never invested a dime of my own. That's the power of leveraging and of silent partners. Enough said!"

I agree.

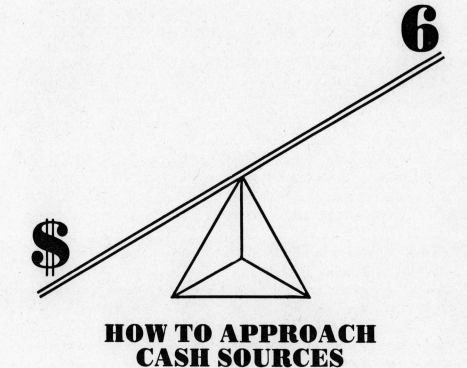

HOW TO APPROACH
CASH SOURCES

Now it's time to sink our teeth into something we have been touching on over and over again throughout the previous chapters. That is the importance of knowing how to properly approach cash sources. Knowing where to look for loans, equity and the like is only one part of your offensive strategy. Equally important is to learn how to present yourself, your business associates, your company and your prospects to those who may provide money for your ventures. Since we are dealing with human beings, not computers, the style of presentation can have as much to do with getting the funds as the hard financial facts. When it comes to seeking business capital, the company does not speak for itself! You must do that, and you must do a damn good job of it to get that cash flowing.

A few things to bear in mind: First, never forget that you are not the only one seeking business funds. The commercial world is crowded with entrepreneurs with good ideas and promising companies who are out to drum up money. In most cases, the sources you approach for cash hear many appeals every day or week of the year. They've heard it all before, have had their share of losers, have been burned once or twice and are therefore wary of how and where they invest. What they are looking for, more than anything else, is that one prospective deal that really shines—stands out from the others and commands attention. It is your job, therefore, as a leveraged entrepreneur, to make your offer take on this irresistible quality.

How is this done. Here's one good approach:

"I always meet a prospective lender or investor with the attitude that they need me more than I need them," says Carlton K. of Mt. Kisco, N.Y., an extremely successful business owner, who has parlayed borrowed funds into a string of used car lots stretching from New Orleans to Miami and all the way north to Boston. "I adopted this frame of mind from the first day I sought cash, even though I didn't have a nickel of my own and needed to get that borrowed money badly.

"But the feeling behind my actions was that it's easy to lend money but it's difficult and rare to come up with a superb way to make money. I knew that my concept for used car lots in major shopping centers was a winner and that anyone who had the 'privilege' to invest in it would make a fortune. So I approached these investors with the attitude that I would decide whom I would allow to invest with me—I'd put them on the defensive. And it worked, I actually had eleven offers to lend all the money I needed and was therefore able to shop around for the best terms."

There's no doubt about it: people like to associate with winners and part of Carlton's success in raising funds can be traced to his work in developing a winning image. To do this, he actually borrowed money and bought a $350 suit, a $75 derby hat and a $150 leather at-tache case. What's more, he printed up lavishly embossed business cards, even though the firm was only an idea at the time. But the stunt worked: "Wherever I went to look for money, I looked like a man who had already made tons of it. People respect that, are intrigued by it and want to be partners with you from the day they lay eyes on you. I guess the old saying is true that the best way to make a million is to look like you've already made it. I've made more than $6 million now, but the first time I walked into the Citizen's Bank with my $350 suit, I was wearing all the assets that I had."

What makes your image so important is that your cash sources will not automatically share your enthusiasm for the business idea, invention or expansion. All too many entrepreneurs make the mis-take of thinking that everyone they talk with will be as excited as they are about the project. But that's not true. Remember, as we have said, most of these investors are inundated with prospective deals: they can't get excited about every one. Also, you are the one who has developed the idea, played around with it, recognized its pos-sibilities. Since it is your brainstorm, the fires of imagination are in your mind at first, no one else's. Not that the investors can't come around to be equally enthusiastic. If you do your job of presenting well, they will be. But not at first. So your image as winner will have to carry you until the point in your discussions where you can really illustrate the potential of your business idea. Unless you can "hook" the investor with your successful appearance and style, you may never get to second base. Come in looking like a loser and your cash source may dismiss you right off the bat.

The following is a list of psychological pointers to keep in mind when approaching potential investors:

1. Always dress in a formal business suit, the more expensive the better, even if meeting at the individual's home, club or favorite restaurant. It is, in fact, to your advantage to be dressed more elaborately than the other party: this gives you a psychological edge.

2. Imply that you have a number of potential offers lined up, and are simply shopping around for the best terms to suit "you."

3. Never let on that you are desperate. Appear this way to the investor and you will be treated like a beggar, undeserving of his time or attention.

4. Exhibit great confidence in your business or idea. Start off your conversation with the most dramatic point that you can make. It is a mistake to save the best for last: you may have lost the person by then.

5. Be reserved. Tell no more about your venture then you absolutely must. This makes the source believe that to get the inside facts, he will have to be part of the team—committed as a full-fledged investor.

6. Leave the meeting with an air of confidence. Tell the potential investor to call "you" when he's had a chance to review the proposal—do not volunteer to call him. Say that you are off to another business meeting and imply that you are an exceptionally busy person.

7. Leave a business card. This is always much more effective than simply jotting down your number on a piece of scratch paper. Even if you can't afford $100 for fancy cards, go to a discount printer and get them for $10. It is a must.

Every specific plan of action for approaching capital sources must be custom-tailored to the precise type of group, organization or individual you will be meeting. Different investors think and act differently, look for different things for and from their investments and operate in different ways. So, just how you will position yourself and your venture depends on whom you will be meeting. It is therefore a good idea to learn as much as possible about each investor before making personal contact. If it's a family venture capitalist you are going to see, try to speak with others who have worked with the person in the past. Is he a conservative dresser? Does he have certain strong political views? Is he patient, or does he like a brief and prompt presentation? Knowing all of this in advance can prevent you from wearing the wrong color tie, making the gauche statement about Republicans or speaking longer than the other party likes. And, since all investors are human, tripping up in one of these areas can turn them off to you as a business owner even though your faux pas has nothing to do with business. It happens to be true, even if irrational, that investors are most likely to put up their money for people they like.

Doing research into prospective lenders and investors also saves you the time and effort of going after the wrong sources. Some institutions and individuals are simply not interested in dealing with small ventures—they prefer to work only with large, well established firms. Knowing your sources well makes you a much more effective leveraged entrepreneur. This is especially true when dealing with one of the most important sources of financing: banks.

THE DIFFERENCES AMONG BANKS

To all too many small business owners, a bank is a bank is a bank. Behind the catchy advertising jingles and the giveaways, the general impression is that banks are one and the same: cold, aloof and impersonal.

The age-old image of the friendly, neighborhood banker has become a bit tarnished over the years. No longer viewed as pillars of the financial community, banks are held in low esteem by millions of Americans. Many small companies, in fact, view banks as hostile institutions, closely allied with big corporate interests.

"The problem is that an entrepreneur remains loyal to a bank for many years, giving a single branch all of his commercial business," says F.P. Longeway, vice president of the National Small Business Association. "Then when the entrepreneur suddenly needs a loan, more often than not the bank acts like they don't even know him. In many cases, banks are willing to turn their backs on small business customers just when these customers need help the most."

This kind of negative experience leads many owner-managers to judge all banks by the policies of a few. This, however, is taking the easy way out. Banks, like the customers they serve, differ in many ways. Entrepreneurs taking the time to shop around may find a local bank deeply committed to working with the small business community.

"Banking is a two-way street," says a spokesman for the American Bankers Association. "Small business people have to learn what they can and can not expect from banks before they can ever hope to establish satisfactory bank relationships.

"What's more, those who lump all banks together miss an important point: banks are competitive. Although most banks may look alike, they do offer different services—do stress different policies. The only way to know, however, where a bank stands, is to ask. Small business owners must survey the banks in their communities, doing a little research to determine which banks offer the most appealing services. It's like shopping for anything else: a little preparation on the customer's part can yield a substantial return in the long run.''

Is your bank aware of small business problems? Does it cater to small business customers? Does the branch provide adequate business services? Does another bank in town offer more? Do you know how to build a solid banking relationship? Do you know how to boost the odds of getting a loan?

Experts offer the following guidelines for finding, rating and utilizing bank services:

- Ask if there is a loan officer specializing in small business financing. An officer familiar with small business needs is most likely to grant loan approval.

- Make a comparison of available loan terms. Compare the different banks in terms of interest rates, loan periods, compensating balance requirements and how much they are willing to lend.

- Find out what kind of collateral the bank requires for business loans. Will you have to pledge all or part of your business assets? Will personal property be involved? Even banks on the same street may differ widely on collateral requirements.

- Look for the bank that offers the widest range of business-related services such as computerized payroll accounts, free checking for your employees and international currency transfers.

- Also, select a bank with experience in personal financial services for the self-employed such as estate and trust management, automatic savings and bond custody. Many banks, for example, will supervise customer bond holdings, clip the coupons and put the proceeds into special accounts.

- Try to work with a single commercial bank. Splitting the business only divides loyalty and hampers credibility.

- When seeking a loan, prepare a projection showing what your business situation will be following the injection of new capital.

Project sales and profits for the term of the loan and prepare a cash flow statement to show when profits will repay the loan.

- Invite the banker to your place of business. Be open and candid, revealing everything the officer should know about your operations.

Once you get down to brass tacks with your lender or investor, you must retain the feeling of security and strength that you used in the first meeting. Do anything less and you'll be taken for a ride. Being a successful entrepreneur demands that you get your funds under the best possible terms—and that involves the art and science of negotiation. Again, dealing with banks provides a good example of what this entails and what you must look out for.

Remember that in business, learning the hard way means making mistakes, taking your lumps and trying again. For business owners, the payoff comes in being wiser and more experienced the second time around.

This education by trial and error is common to every company. Even the most talented managers can not hope to do everything right. The problem is, some errors can have devastating repercussions—severe enough to haunt a firm for years after the blunder is made. This is especially true of those mistakes involving business loans.

Small business borrowers usually focus on only one aspect of loans: getting the most money lenders will allow. This is myopic. Although the funds may be granted, the terms of the loan may prove to be detrimental to the firm's growth and development. In these days of rising interest rates, for example, many small firms are learning that their outstanding loans are suddenly costing more to repay. Escalator clauses allow the lender to boost debt service as the prime interest rate increases.

The keys to successful borrowing are to understand lending terminology, to be familiar with the kinds of loans available and to learn to negotiate for the best possible terms. This three-pronged program can put the firm on sound footing from the start.

"Small companies need not approach the loan market with their tails between their legs," says a loan officer with a major national bank. "By acting as if they would be grateful for any kind of loan they can get, these companies put the ball entirely in the lender's court—

and some lenders take advantage of this. They force the borrower to accept what are really unfavorable terms.''

Granted, small firms will never have the clout of the Fortune 500—and many can not afford to be too selective in seeking a cooperative loan source—but by changing their emphasis from ''getting'' a loan to ''negotiating'' for one, they can save thousands of dollars in interest charges, reduce the amount of collateral or obtain other benefits.

In many cases, it is a matter of psychology: approach the lenders in a secure and professional manner and you are less likely to be treated as an easy mark. For one reason or another, many financial institutions want to do business with small companies—it can be profitable and can lead to good community relations. So don't think they are doing you a favor.

The following information can help borrowers negotiate the best possible loans:

1. Some banks are now offering two-tier loan programs, extending the lowest interest rates (even below the prime rate) to small companies. Although this is not a widespread practice, it may be negotiated on an individual basis. The borrower must, however, be knowledgeable and confident enough to ask for it.

2. The ''covenants'' section of a loan agreement spells out the restrictions you will have to live with as part of the deal. Negative covenants are things the borrower may not do without prior approval from the lender. Some examples are: additions to the borrower's total debt and the issuance of excess dividends. Positive covenants, on the other hand, spell out the things the borrower must do. This may include the maintenance of minimum net working capital and carrying adequate insurance. Make certain that you can accept these covenants—or try to get the lender to compromise on some of them— before signing on the dotted line.

3. Of the two major types of short-term bank financing—secured and unsecured loans—it is best to try for the latter. Unsecured loans do not require collateral: the bank relies on your credit reputation.

AN APPROACH TO GOVERNMENT SOURCES

Approaching government loan sources can be somewhat different, because the approval procedure tends to be less arbitrary.

Many government loan officers go by the book, so to speak, meaning that they expect things to be done in a certain way and no alternatives will suffice. That's the bureaucratic mentality and it's what you will have to learn to cater to and deal with when seeking government-related financing.

In these cases, the best approach is to determine precisely what the government agency expects and then follow it to the "T". That is really the safest way to approach this type of cash source. How should you apply for a Small Business Administration loan, for example? Well, here's what the SBA itself suggests:

1. Prepare a current financial statement or balance sheet (see Chapter 9) listing all assets and all liabilities of the business—do not include personal items.

2. Have an earnings (profit and loss) statement for the previous full year and for the current period to date.

3. Prepare a current personal financial statement of the owner, or each partner or stockholder owning 20 percent or more of the corporate stock in the business.

4. List collateral to be offered as security for the loan, with your estimate of the current market value of each item.

5. State amount of loan requested and explain exact purposes for which it will be used.

6. Take this material with you and see your banker. Ask for a direct bank loan and, if denied, ask the bank to make the loan under the SBA's Loan Guaranty Plan or to participate with the SBA in a loan. If the bank is interested in an SBA guarantee or participation loan, ask the banker to contact the SBA for discussion of your application.

7. If a guaranty or participation loan is not available, write or visit the nearest SBA office. The SBA has 96 field offices and, in addition, sends loan officers to visit many smaller cities on a regularly scheduled basis or as the need is indicated. To speed matters, make your financial information available when you first write or visit the SBA.

For new businesses, the SBA procedure is different:

1. Describe in detail the kind of business to be established.

2. Describe experience and management capabilities.

3. Prepare an estimate of how much you or others have to invest in the business and how much you will need to borrow.

4. Prepare a current financial statement listing all personal assets and all liabilities.

5. Prepare a detailed projection of earnings for the first year the business will operate.

6. List collateral to be offered as security for the loan, indicating your estimate of the present market value of each item.

Steps 7 and 8 are the same as those listed previously for established firms.

The procedures for dealing with venture capital firms are less rigid than those which are appropriate for government agencies. Still, however, there is the right way and the wrong way to get things done. Although venture capitalists differ in their investment criteria and objectives, most tend to judge entrepreneurs according to similar standards. Knowing how to live up to these standards vastly improves your chances of getting money.

What is the best strategy to adopt? Well, we think that following these steps will help to make your proposal most attractive to the venture capital community:

• Do not let it be known that you have a list of venture capital firms to visit and that the company you are presenting your ideas to is just one of many. Any inkling that yours is a losing idea—that others have heard and rejected it—will damage you severely. Venturists are alike in that all want to be the first to hear of a hot new product or service; they want first crack at discovering a potential gold mine. Give them any idea that your proposal has already been rejected by others and the promise of success is removed immediately.

This is not to say that venturists will never take on projects turned down by their peers—they do it all the time. And we do not advocate distorting the truth about who else has reviewed your project or proposal. But what is undeniable is that it is best to position your proposal as fresh and original. Don't talk about your visits with other venturists, and don't let previous rejections give you a defeatist attitude that others can detect.

• It is invaluable to have your initial contact with the venture capitalists arranged through the offices of a well-regarded investment banker, commercial banker, attorney, accountant or entrepreneur who has dealt successfully with the venture firm. This go-between serves as a first reference for you and makes you stand out from the many others (as we have noted) who are applying for financing simultaneously.

Be aware, however, that those parties introducing you to the venture capitalists—and this is especially true for investment banks—often charge a finder's fee should you be successful in arranging the deal. It is my opinion that this is money well worth spent. Remember, as a leveraged entrepreneur you must think big. Getting bogged down in petty fee considerations is not what will make you successful.

In line with this, the cheapest way to contact venture capitalists is the way that offers the least hope of ever getting financing. This involves sending a mass mailing to a list of venture firms, outlining your credentials and business plans. This kind of unsolicited mail gets little attention.

• Prepare a detailed proposal of your business plan to review in person with the venture capitalists and to leave behind for them to study further. This should be between 20 and 25 pages, professionally typed on crisp white bond (using a letterhead is best) or high-quality copy paper (never use coated copy paper).

The proposal should answer all the initial questions venturists may have about your background, business idea and potential for success. They will not base their investment decision solely on this but will use it to determine whether or not to proceed with a more comprehensive analysis.

THE "FIRST DATE" WITH INVESTORS

"To put it in simple social terms, entrepreneurs should think of the proposal as a first date," says the president of an active east coast venture firm. "Both parties want to see if they are interested in each other, if they turn each other on, so to speak, and if they want this to develop into a meaningful relationship or if it's only a one-night stand. Just as a man or woman can often tell through that first date interaction if there's any potential for the relationship, we can often determine the same, from an investment point of view, from the entrepreneur's proposal."

Effective proposals provide a clear picture of the management capabilities and experience of the entrepreneurs seeking financing. The impression that their investment will be in capable hands is the most important single thing that you can relate to the venturists.

In those cases where the investment opportunity involves an invention, new technology or highly-complex manufacturing capabilities, the proposal should illustrate clearly and effectively that the related product will perform as promised. This should be done with the use of blueprints, engineering reports, technical drawings, chemical analyses and whatever else will lend scientific authority to your plan or idea.

"I've always found that a statement by a respected engineering or testing firms as to the plausibility of the project in question influenced me in favor of backing it," says the president of the venture capital firm. "I'm not an engineer so I have to rely on those professional opinions that I trust in order to determine if, in fact, the project has merit. The entrepreneurs who really know how to approach cash sources build this kind of credibility into their proposals."

It is a good idea, then, to ask an objective source of expert information to make a positive statement on your technical presentation and to include this in the proposal. This will impress the venture capitalists that you are a good enough business manager to pay attention to the vital details.

A winning proposal should also contain an in-depth discussion of your marketing plans. Although you are not expected to be a marketing genius, you must present clear ideas on your proposed distribution system, suggested prices and most of all, competition. What is the nature of existing or potential competition in your field, industry or product classification? Will you have the strength to get established in light of the competition and will you have what it takes to grow when competition mounts a serious challenge?

The worst thing that you can do when discussing competition is to try to hide the extent of your competitor's strength from the venture capitalists. If there is a competitive threat, they will find out about it. It is their business, after all, to spot every possible problem well before they come up with the big bucks. Let them find something important that you've failed to report (something you tried to camouflage) and you'll look like a poor businessman—one who does not even know his own market. The best approach to presenting the facts about competition is to be clear and honest and to tell how, in fact, you would manage to knock off competitors. Even giants like Proctor & Gamble take their lumps from smaller companies now and then. Show how you would do it and you'll get a fair hearing, but act as if Proctor & Gamble doesn't exist and you'll look like a fool.

The whole science of business marketing has come to the fore in recent years, especially with venture capitalists. Marketing is more than just salesmanship: it is the function that bridges production and consumption. Marketers must be familiar with the characteristics of consumer or industrial demand, the mechanics of distribution and the formulas for pricing products so that they are both profitable and competitive. Demonstrating some knowledge of modern marketing will surely win points with the venture capitalists. If you yourself are not adept at marketing, hire an executive or a consultant to work with you in this field—and make it clear that you have this help in your proposal.

Finally, the proposal should include some discussion of how the projected financing will be put to use. Venturists want to know how you intend to spend the money you are seeking. This allows them to gauge whether or not your budgets are realistic, if you will have enough money or are asking for more than you need and if you have some knowledge of business finances. At least part of your financial treatment should include a rough percentage budget for the funds you will raise:

COMPANY ABC
VENTURE CAPITAL FINANCING $1 MILLION
BREAKDOWN OF EXPENDITURES

PRODUCTION OF FIRST 500 UNITS	$300,000
NEW PERSONNEL	$100,000
ACQUISITION OF FIXED ASSETS	$200,000
IMPROVEMENTS IN PHYSICAL PLANT	$150,000
SG&A	$150,000
ADVERTISING AND PROMOTION	$100,000

We also recommend devoting up to a full page of your proposal on the financial controls you plan to implement. What systems will be used to verify invoices? Who will be allowed to approve or authorize company checks? Who will audit the company's books? If international sales are involved, what measures will be taken to account for currency fluctuations and to protect the firm from losses in this area? Some sign that you are taking tough financial controls will be viewed as a mark of professionalism by the venturers.

You now have a clear picture of what it takes to successfully approach a number of important cash sources. You know that different strategies are required for different types of investors. Just how you play your cards depends, to a great extent, on whom you are seeking money from.

ONE KEY STRATEGIC ELEMENT

There is one aspect of the entrepreneurial presentation that remains the same, however, regardless of the loan or investment source. That is, the importance of stressing your own management capabilities. Of all the prerequisites for securing outside financing—especially in substantial sums—proving that you are worth your salt as a business owner-manager is the most crucial.

For this reason, I suggest that you prepare what I call a "Prime Borrower's Profile." This is a professional resume outlining your personal qualities, characteristics and experience—the factors that indicate your capabilities as an entrepreneur. As I have said, the investors may not know too much about your specific business or product but if they can be convinced of your abilities, they are more likely to invest with you.

When preparing your "Prime Borrower's Profile" stress your on-the-job experience as a business owner or manager. This so-called track record is what investors and lenders are most interested in. Don't be humble here. If you have been a winner in all previous ventures—if the companies' successes were due entirely to you—say so loud and clear. Of next greatest importance is quality academic credentials. Obviously, a high school diploma is nothing to brag about, but if you have business degrees (especially a Master of

Business Administration) list all the details in prominent fashion. The better the reputation of the schools, the more impact this will have. Finally, personal factors such as character references and credit standing should be included. Try to get references from those who can attest to your business acumen—bankers, lawyers and entrepreneurs are especially good for this. And tell them to be specific in their references; not just that "John Smith is a hell of a guy," but more like "John Smith has proven to me, during a stint of employment at my company, that he is the finest conceptual merchandiser of women's fashions that I have ever seen." Remember, you are not out to win a personality contest. Your goal is to prove your abilities as a business owner.

Not every applicant for business funds has a well-rounded background featuring top schools, an impressive track record and contacts with the local bank president. And that certainly does not disqualify you from getting the necessary funds. What you should do, however, is to design the "Prime Borrower's Profile" to emphasize your strengths. Entrepreneurs with a fine record of running profitable companies but who never got beyond the sixth grade (and there are many like this), should play up their business experience and completely eliminate education. It does more harm than good.

"Prime Borrower Profiles" are recommended for use in approaching every type of cash source from SBA to commercial banks to venture capitalists. The following is a sample Profile which can be used as a guide in preparing your own:

PRIME BORROWER'S PROFILE

John A. Smith
123 Main St.
New York, N.Y. 10017   212 666 6666

Entrepreneurial Experience

Founder and president of ACME Widgets, a $9 million annual revenues firm producing and marketing widgets throughout the U.S. and Canada. Established in 1961, the firm now employs 350 people and enjoys a growth rate of 21 percent per year (average).

Senior Vice President of A1 Widgets, a St. Louis based firm which is the world's largest widget producer. Held full executive responsibility for international marketing through a field sales force of more than 500 representatives. Served 1950 to 61.

Education

Columbia University, 1970 to present, continuing education in the graduate business school in all areas of business finance including accounting and international finance.

Harvard University, Masters of Business Administration (major concentration in marketing), class of 1944. Graduated with the highest grade point average of 450 students in the business school.

Stanford University, class of 1941, B.S. Degree in Business Management. Cumulative Grade average of A—, eight semesters on the Dean's List for superior achievement and captain of the swim team.

References

William A. Williams, current president of A1 Widgets.

Barton A. Barton, assistant corporate counsel for the City of New York

Wallace A. Wallace, president, First N.Y. Bank of Manhattan.

Personal

Age 57   Married, three children   Perfect Health

"I was very wary of being able to raise money from sophisticated investors because my education never went beyond grade school," says Morris F., president of Morris Accounting Services. "I had to quit school in junior high in order to help pay the bills when my father passed away. Although this was certainly a legitimate reason, I was smart enough to know that investors want proof of your abilities, not hard luck stories."

Persuaded by his son, a vice president of the firm, that Morris Accounting could grow from its base of five offices (providing accounting and tax services to small business and individuals) into a major regional company, Morris approached investors in spite of his educational shortcomings.

"I knew that a man like dad, who started with nothing and built a thriving business with pure smarts and ambition—a man who had no degree in accounting but had 45 accountants on his payroll—could overcome the educational limitation and make investors believe in him anyway. To do this, I had him use a resume of his experience, listing in great detail how he had founded and nurtured Morris Accounting to a $4 million a year business.''

Son Rob, a Yale Law School graduate, prepared his father's Prime Borrower's Profile. That was back in 1972.

''In this case, son, not father, knew best,'' Morris admits, beaming all the while. ''The very first cash source I approached, accompanied by Rob, of course, was Galaxy Investors of New Haven, Conn., a relatively small venture capital firm. They were specialists in service businesses, were very impressed with my track record and agreed to come up with a package worth $3 million to open seven new offices to start. They never said a word about my education until our third meeting—and by then they were hooked on Morris, the businessman. I had proved I was a success without a degree.''

Today, Morris' firm has 63 offices, annual revenues of $45 million and two sons and a daughter who are vice presidents.

It's not always easy to get business financing, but if you know how to get around the obstacles it can almost always be done. Learning the proper ways to approach cash sources is a real plus.

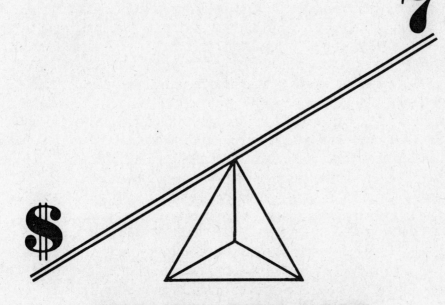

HOW TO LOOK GOOD
ON PAPER: PREPARING
DOCUMENTS THAT SWAY
LENDERS AND INVESTORS

The men and women who are cut out to be leveraged entrepreneurs have a tendency to think big. The ability to arrange and implement major business deals is the aptitude most needed for success in this endeavor. Leveraging is not for the cautious, conservative, balanced-budget types who are content to grow at a snail's pace. Not at all. Leveraged finance attracts those individuals who want to start or expand a business to major proportions. For them, starting a candy store or local newspaper delivery service is not the dream: that's for the small thinkers. Leveraged entrepreneurs specializing in start-up situations have in mind chains of stores, major factories, national distribution and huge enterprises. And those established business owners now taking the leveraged route will not be content with expanding their operations by 10 or 15 percent. No—you don't need leveraging for that. Internal financing can handle that kind of expansion just fine.

The established entrepreneurs who turn to leveraging want to double the size of their companies, at the very least, and they want that growth to come within a few years. There is a price to pay for this kind of grandiose planning and that is the need to attract substantial financing. The person just getting started in business is unlikely to have the personal funds required to launch a major enterprise from the start. And the owner of one or two shops is rarely capable of bankrolling enough from previous profits to open 20 more stores.

This, of course, supports the theme I have been stressing throughout: that it takes big money to make it big in business, but that the money does not have to be your own. Investors and lenders in the private and governmental sectors are ready and waiting to fund promising ventures in all stages of development. What you have to do is to position your venture as one that is worthy of the financial risks involved. You now know that this takes a considerable amount of preparation, planning and sophistication. Nothing materially good in this world is easy to get: to attract the tremendous amounts of capital that you want, effort must be put into the process.

We have discussed the proper way to approach cash sources and how to use psychological factors to boost the odds of obtaining leveraged financing. Once you have progressed this far, however, you must go the next step, which is working with the financial documents and applications that are so closely scrutinized by investors. The emphasis here is on hard financial information: Those firms and individuals seeking capital must be prepared to prove that their companies will succeed, repay the loans, provide investors with a reasonable yield, and achieve a solid growth record. You must now go beyond the "Prime Borrower's Profile," and beyond the initial proposal, to a more in-depth and factual presentation.

THE "BUSINESS PLAN"

Let's start off with what I call "The Business Plan." For the purposes of obtaining large sums of money, the formal Business Plan should be an elaborate version of the Business Proposal (discussed in Chapter 6). If you think of the Business Proposal as a skeleton, the Business Plan puts the meat on the bones. Rather than a sort of outline, it is a comprehensive review of your business and its projected performance. The following elements should be included in an effective Business Plan:

A Discussion of any Special Issues Which Are Currently Affecting the Business or Industry You Are in or Are Seeking to Enter. Certain social, political or cultural influences may seem to be working for or against your field: the business plan should make mention of them. Entrepreneurs now considering entry into the fast food field, for example, must contend with a number of pressing factors. First, there is concern in the investment community that many communities are now saturated with McDonald's, Burger King, Arthur Treacher's and the like and that there are decreasing opportunities to succeed in this market.

Entrepreneurs seeking funds for this type of venture must provide investors with some form of USP (Unique Selling Point), which is that characteristic of a business that makes it stand out from the competition. This can be done very effectively: A number of upstarts have given Kentucky Fried Chicken serious competition in many major markets, even though it once seemed that KFC had this part of the fast food industry locked up.

Another problem in the fast food industry has to do with environmental regulations and zoning restrictions. Angered by unsanitary conditions and unsightly facilities, many communities are saying "no" to zoning requests for new fast food outlets and others have banned this kind of establishment completely. Investors are known to fear that this rising sentiment will effect a slow growth in the industry in the coming decade.

Issues such as these have their counterparts in most every in dustry. We live in an age of increasing restraints on business operations: diminishing natural resources, pollution controls, inflation and consumerism. Just how this will affect your venture should be discussed in the Business Plan. Not a full treatise on the subject, to be sure, but simply enough to signal your awareness of the problem and to soothe investor fears, pointing out that the trouble is not too great to handle.

The best approach is to explain briefly how you would tackle the problem. Back to the fast food example. It is best to anticipate investor fears about zoning restrictions and to line up a number of acceptable locations before the Business Plan is presented. Give the names and addresses of the areas in which you have some assurance that you can build. Indicate how you got that assurance, and why the locations will be good from a marketing standpoint as well. If you can include statements from the zoning boards that there is no objection, in principle, to fast food outlets, this can be a real plus. Similar strategies should be used for problems in other businesses.

Give Some Historical Perspective to Your Venture. If you are entering an established industry, briefly trace its origins, early development, recent trends and current status. Most important are any developments which have changed the status quo by diminishing established markets and opening new opportunities. The women's apparel business has been revolutionized in recent years by a shift away from couture clothing (limited edition designer collections with price tags of $1000 and up) to an overwhelming concentration on quality ready-to-wear fashions. Only a handful of the top designers, like Bill Blass, still bother to produce a couture line and he does it not for the profits but for the prestige it can add to his ready-to-wear clothes. There simply is no longer a significant market for couture fashions. Entrepreneurs seeking capital for ready-to-wear production should make note of this change in the market.

A Business Plan for a new invention should devote some space to the behind-the-scenes development of the product. Why did the inventor think a market would exist for it? Is he filling a legitimate consumer or industrial need?

This is a crucial distinction. Many individuals are scientists first, business owners second. They invent new products simply for the thrill of invention, of discovery. This is fine in a university setting, or for a hobby, but it is not good enough for investors or money lenders. In most cases, these people do not give a damn about the scientific breakthrough unless it has real commercial value. The

Business Plan must relate science to business. Coming up with a sure-fire way to manufacture light bulbs that never burn out is useless commercially if the materials required for this demand that the bulbs sell for a minimum of $900 each. Consumers simply will not buy them.

Food processors, on the other hand, are an example of a product invention which proved to have strong commercial appeal. The Business Plan for such products revealed the facts that increasing numbers of women were becoming interested in cooking again, that elaborate dishes were popular in many households and that kitchen appliance sales—especially blenders—were at record levels. What the inventor did was to combine the trend towards cooking, with the popularity of existing appliances, to develop a new type of equipment that went one step further than what was already on the market. Rather than simply blending foods, processors whip, grate, cut, chop and mix.

"The processors were really a product line whose time had come," says the kitchen wares manager of a major New York department store. "Not only do they help budding cooks make better meals, but they also help them to do it all much faster. This means that the career woman who wants to cook can do her job and her hobby well."

This kind of market rationale for a product, especially a new and untested one, should go into the Business Plan. Try to get those who would be involved in selling the product—like a top buyer at Sears— to state his desire to sell it. This will give lenders and investors great confidence in the marketability of the product. Include the names and affiliations of those giving testimonials in the Business Plan.

Mention Anything Which Makes Your Product, Company or Service Exclusive and Somewhat Impervious to Competition. Trade secrets, patents and exclusive distributor rights, for example, are viewed as being extremely valuable. Although you should not, especially in the negotiating stages, reveal secret information, it is a good idea to list patent numbers and some general details about distribution agreements.

Devote a Section to Market Research. Here, you will need more than the brief overview of the market used in the initial proposal. The research section of the formal Business Plan must illustrate that you (or a consulting agency hired by you) have conducted some in-depth studies of the market in which you will be selling. This falls into two categories of information: quantitative and qualitative. The first is what is frequently referred to as a "market measurement" study. That is, how big is the market and how much is it likely to grow (its elasticity). Investors will expect you to come up with documented statistics.

Simply stating that "the market for color television sets in Cincinnati will always be great because people there like to watch a lot of television and the city's population is constantly growing," is not nearly enough factual information to satisfy sophisticated financiers, bankers and the like. To get to first base, your approach will have to be more like this, "According to the latest Bureau of the Census Reports, only 36 percent of Cincinnati households have color televisions. A poll conducted by our company reveals that of those families without color sets, 78 percent plan to buy one in the next two years. Based on this information and the projected rate of replacement for existing sets, we anticipate a 50 percent increase in sales in 1980 through 82."

In gathering market research statistics for the Business Plan, entrepreneurs can turn to "primary" and "secondary" sources. Primary sources are those which are custom tailored to your research needs. These include polls, consumer interviews, and Q&A forms sent to prospective retailers or suppliers. If you are entering an especially risky type of business—or one that has not been tested before—it is worth the expense to conduct such research on your own or to pay specialists to do it for you. There are a number of leading firms that do this work for a fee (ask your trade association or banker for names). Research through secondary sources, which can also be very reliable and accurate, can be done at little or no expense. This involves using published materials as your sources of data. The Wall Street Journal, for example, runs regular stories on the findings of the Conference Board, an organization which studies various aspects of our economy, including the levels of consumer confidence. And the Census Bureau, probably the best source for free and low-cost market research information, provides a wealth of data on businesses, consumers and geographical markets. Research into the prospects for your venture can be done through Census Reports and then reported in your Business Plan. For a list of all available Census reports write for the Catalog of Census Bureau Publications, Bureau of the Census, Washington, D.C.

"My dream from childhood was to open a chain of gardening centers—the kind that would sell nursery products but would also send gardeners to private homes to provide complete services there as well—planting, cutting, seeding, mowing and so on," says Dom P. of Saginaw, Mich. "I proved my abilities to succeed in the business by founding and building two hugely-successful centers that generated more than $3 million in annual receipts. I had a few dollars of my own bankrolled in the old business kitty and had seven additional sites all picked out for new stores. To break ground, however, I estimated that I needed $2.1 million from the banks. They were enthusiastic about my ideas and my track record, but wanted some additional research on the wisdom of my selected sites. Would they be able to generate the kind of volume my existing centers turned in?"

To get the answers ("to tell the truth, I wanted to know as much as they did," Dom adds), Dom checked out the Census on Population and Housing for the communities he planned to build in. The reports show the number of residents in the areas and the percentage of that total population that lives in single-family housing.

"This told us how big our market was around each prospective site," Dom adds. "Once we had that, we simply checked out how many garden centers were already in the area. As long as there was less than one existing nursery per each 10,000 population, we felt confident that we could proceed—and so did the banks. In only one of the sites did we fail to meet that criteria, so we scrapped the plans for that one. In the others, however, we found that there was less than one nursery per 20,000 population. That was all the banks had to see— the money came flowing in."

Include a Discussion of Promotional Strategies. Indicate the media that will be used and the percentage of the total budget slated for television, radio, billboards, newspapers, magazines and direct mail. If the campaign will be produced by an advertising agency, name the firm and give the reasons for its selection.

Some ventures lend themselves well to public relations campaigns. This is the kind of thing investors appreciate, because public relations work is generally much less expensive than advertising. A dramatic new invention, for example, will be able to generate substantial publicity and this may get the ball rolling in terms of distributor involvement and consumer acceptance. So try to make some provision in the Business Plan for public relations.

The Business Plan should be about three times as long as the initial proposal—about 60 to 75 pages will do. Any less will not be enough to cover all of the essentials in sufficient detail; any more will read like a book, and that can bore the busy investor. It is necessary, therefore, to strike a delicate balance.

Another good device is to start the Plan off with a four-page summary of its most salient features. This thumbnail sketch of your Plan will entice interested lenders and investors to read on. Be sure this section is especially well written. The old saying about first impressions being the most important holds true—and the summary is the first thing readers will see.

A KEY DOCUMENT

Another key document you will need to obtain big-league financing is the so-called "cash flow projection." Put simply, it charts the flow of cash in and out of a company. Most importantly, it shows precisely when there will be inflows and when there will be outflows. The importance of this is clear: Management must know that there will always be sufficient cash coming in to meet all expenses, including payroll, raw materials, production, promotion and so forth.

The cash flow projection is especially vital for a new business, because in these cases it often takes some time for the inflow to match outflow and even longer still for the level of profits to be big enough to finance the firm's expansion. And this is clearly what investors and lenders want to know from the cash flow projection: When is the venture likely to be able to start repaying its debts and stand on its own?

In many cases, the analysis for a start-up venture or a business expansion does not prove that the business will be profitable in "X" amount of years, but show instead that it will never achieve acceptable profitability. An idea for a company or product that may seem to be a winner in theory may prove to be a dog on paper.

This is why the money men demand projections from those entrepreneurs seeking funds. If the venture will not yield a satisfactory return within a reasonable amount of time, they do not want any part of it. Although this may sound, at first, like an arrogant precaution, it really is not. Every investor has the right to hedge his bets and look for some assurance of return. What's more, the cash flow projection also protects the entrepreneur who is seeking funds. If your idea has little hope of generating sufficient cash, why waste your time and efforts on it either.

Your cash flow projection should be prepared by a Certified Public Accountant. It is not something that should be tackled by a novice. After all, those who will study the projection are certain to be accountants and other financial experts. Still, it is a good idea for you, as the responsible entrepreneur, to understand the mechanics of a cash flow projection.

The projection should be done on a single large sheet of paper. It should cover a period of from three to five years, with the first year broken down into monthly installments and the balance shown monthly or quarterly. The major components of the projection are:

The Beginning Cash Balance

Add to this—Bank loans
> **Proceeds from the sale of stock**
> **Cash receipts**
> **Collection of accounts receivable**
> **Other receipts**

> **This Gives the Total Receipts**

Subtract from this—Income taxes
> **Loan repayments**
> **Expenses for sales, promotions, manufacturing, labor, general and administrative**
> **Fixed asset additions**
> **Disbursements**
> **Other payments**

> **This Gives the Total Disbursements**

Finally you have the change in cash position (increase or decrease) and the closing balance.

EXAMINING A COMPREHENSIVE
CASH FLOW ANALYSIS

Let's examine a comprehensive cash flow analysis for a hypothetical company we will call AAA Communications. The founding entrepreneur, a veteran food editor for a national magazine, has left his regular job in order to launch a private newsletter for gourmets across the U.S. The publication, which will be produced monthly for an annual subscription of $30 (less for volume subscription orders), will feature original recipes, restaurant reviews and tips on using kitchen appliances.

The founder has no money of his own to invest but is negotiating a deal with a small advertising agency that may be willing to foot all of the costs in return for a 49 percent interest in the venture. The editor will be providing his reputation in the field, his ability to promote the publication through newspaper and magazine articles that he writes on a regular basis and he will be responsible for the editorial content of the newsletter. The ad agency will have to print and distribute the publication, conduct magazine and direct mail promotion campaigns and pay all of the bills for advertising, postage, facilities and personnel. The deal hinged on the agency's preparation of analyses to determine if, in fact, their investment would yield a reasonable return. The cash flow projection is shown in the tables that follow.

Some explanations are now in order:

- All figures are based on the assumption that of all direct mail promotions and requests for information generated by space advertising and so forth, only one percent of the target consumers will actually order subscriptions. This is a cautious assumption but is not out of line in a business where a five percent positive response is considered to be exceptionally good. One percent is used here because lenders and investors will often insist on the most conservative estimates. They do not want to build their expectation on misleading statistics.

- Negative cash flow (more going out than coming in) occurs during the first few months of the year because this is the time of heaviest promotional expenses, including the bulk of direct mailing.

MONTH	1	2	3	4	5	6
SALES:						
CASH:						
NEWSPAPER		2000	1500	1500	1500	1500
SPACE ADS		1000	2000	500	1000	1000
DIRECT MAIL		12000	12000	6000		
CREDIT:						
SPACE ADS			500	1000	2000	1000
DIRECT MAIL			5000	20000	15000	10000
	0	15000	21000	29000	19500	13500
COSTS:						
PROMOTION	50000					
PRODUCTION	3000	3000	3000	3000	3000	3000
ADMINISTRATION	1500	1500	1500	1500	1500	1500
EDITORIAL	500	500	500	500	500	500
CREDIT CARD			500	2000	1500	1500
TOTAL	55000	5000	5500	7000	6500	6500
NET	(55000)	10000	15500	22000	13000	7000
CUMULATIVE:	(55000)	(45000)	(29500)	(7500)	5500	12500

FIRST YEAR (CONTINUED)

	7	8	9	10	11	12	TOTAL
	1500	1500	1000	1000	1000	1000	15000
	800	300	100	100			3500
							33300
	1000	1000	500				7000
	6000	4800	3000	2000	500	300	66600
	9300	7600	4600	3100	1500	1300	125400
	3000	3000	3000	3000	3000	3000	50000
	1500	1500	1500	1500	1500	1500	36000
	500	500	500	500	500	500	18000
					500	500	6000
	1500	1500	1500	1000			12000
	6500	6500	6500	6000	5500	5500	122000
	2800	1100	(1900)	(2900)	(4000)	(4200)	3400
	15300	16400	14500	11600	7600	3400	3400

SECOND YEAR CASH FLOW AT ONE PERCENT RESPONSE

	1	2	3	4	5	6
SALES:						
CASH:						
NEWSPAPER	1250	1250	1250	1250	1250	1250
SPACE ADS		1000	2000	500	1000	1000
DIRECT MAIL		12000	12000	6000	1000	1000
CREDIT						
SPACE ADS			500	1000	2000	1000
DIRECT MAIL			5000	20000	15000	10000
RENEWALS			12000	25000	12000	6000
	1250	14250	32750	53750	31250	19250
costs;						
PROMOTION	50000					
PRODUCTION	4500	4500	4500	4500	4500	4500
ADMIN.	2000	2000	2000	2000	2000	2000
EDITORIAL	750	750	750	750	750	750
CREDIT CARD	200	1000	2500	5000	2500	1000
TOTAL	57450	8250	9750	12250	9750	8250
NET	(56200)	6000	23000	41500	21500	11000
CUMULATIVE	(52800)	(46800)	(23800)	17700	39200	50200

7	8	9	10	11	12	TOTAL
1250	1250	1250	1250	1250	1250	15000
800	300	100	100			3500
						33300
1000	1000	500				7000
6000	4800	3000	2000	500	300	66600
3200	2000	1000	1000	500		62700
12250	9350	5850	4350	2250	1550	188100
4500	4500	4500	4500	4500	4500	50000
2000	2000	2000	2000	2000	2000	54000
750	750	750	750	750	750	24000
1000	500	500	400	200	200	9000
						15000
8250	7750	7750	7650	7450	7450	152000
4000	1600	(1900)	(3300)	(5200)	(5900)	36100
54200	55800	53900	50600	45400	39500	39500

• The provision for credit card costs refers to the fees charged by VISA, American Express, etc. for subscriptions ordered by credit card.

• The editorial fee of $500 and then $750 per month represents initial salary to the editor.

• The direct mailing goes to 115,000 addressees.

• All respondents are offered a free three-month trial period.

• Of those who accept the three month trial, 75 percent choose to receive a full subscription.

• There is a 50 percent renewal rate in the second year.

• Ninety percent of all sales are single subscriptions; the balance are multiple subscriptions ranging from $24 to $18 per subscription.

• Note the strong positive force renewals have on cash flow. Although there is little extra cost to generate this money, renewals make it possible for cash flow to become positive in the fourth month of the second year. In the first year, when there were no renewals, cash flow did not become positive until the fifth month. Even more impressive, positive cash flow reaches $50,000 by the sixth month of the second year vs. $12,500 of the first year.

• The impact of renewals will accelerate even more in subsequent years as the subscriber base grows larger and larger.

"We were convinced, on the strength of the cash flow projection and related financial studies, that the newsletter would be a viable investment—a risk worth taking," says Sally O., senior account executive for the advertising agency.

"What's more, we were so confident about the editorial product catching on with readers that a one-percent response seemed too little," Sally adds. "So, when we based the projections on two percent—which is still rather cautious—positive cash flow reached almost $200,000 by the eighth month of the second year. The business looked very healthy and we were willing to take a shot."

For the founding editor, the decision meant that his firm, AAA Communications, would be financed completely with other people's money. Sure he had to share in the profits, but he was founding a full-fledged, professionally-produced publication without putting up a dime—and they were even paying him a small salary to boot (in addition to his majority stake of the profits).

INCOME STATEMENTS

Cash flow projections, although essential, are not the only financial documents that have such a powerful influence on lenders and investors. Equally important are Income Statements. This is the part of the financial plan that focuses on the amount of profit or loss rather than the raw cash flow. Income Projections help to gauge how profitable a new venture may be, or if it is likely to lose money.

SALES (For New Businesses, Sales and All Other Figures Must Be Estimates)

> **Minus: A Percentage for Bad Debts**
>
> **Minus: Discounts Allowed on Sales**
>
> **Minus: Production Overhead (Utilities, Rent for Facilities, Fringe Benefits, and so forth).**
>
> **Minus: Direct Labor**
>
> **Minus: Cost of Materials**

GROSS PROFIT OR LOSS

> **Less: GS & A (General and Administrative Expenses Including Management, Office Supplies, Accounting and Legal Services.)**
>
> **Less: Sales Expenses**

OPERATING PROFIT OR LOSS

> **Less: Other Expenses not Included Above, Such as Interest**

PRETAX PROFIT OR LOSS

> **Minus: Income Tax Provision**

PROFIT OR LOSS AFTER TAX

For established firms, investors will likely request income statements for the three previous years and projections for three years in advance. Statements should be prepared by accountants, should be on single sheets of ruled paper, and should be broken down the first year by months and in subsequent years by months or quarters.

"The income projections for AAA Communications were also encouraging," says agency account executive Sally O. "Based on a two percent subscription response, which some testing revealed was more realistic than one percent, the newsletter had a projected first year loss of $1300. By the second year, however, we had a net profit projection of $58,350 after taxes; by the third year that zoomed to $73,750. What's more, we were figuring more money for salaries by the third year and still the profits were growing rapidly. By the fourth year the bottom line was projected to climb above $100,000."

The moral of this case history is clear: Serious negotiations with big-money investors and lenders will come to successful fruition only if the entrepreneur is well prepared with the kinds of statistical documents these financiers demand. Hopes, dreams and winning smiles may make you feel good and may help to make friends but they do not produce major financing. Requests for substantial loans or investments must be backed up with documentation that you, your management team, and your business venture have what it takes to succeed.

The best approach is to review all the material in this and the preceding chapters, take a pen and pad and note all of the forms, reports and analyses you will need, ask your banker and accountant what they suggest, compile a master checklist and work with your financial advisers to put together a complete package of supporting materials before you meet with a single cash source.

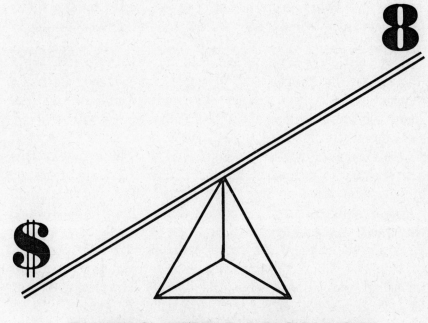

USING THE LANGUAGE
OF LEVERAGING

As a leveraged investor, you must keep in mind that you are now operating in the big leagues. When it comes to attracting significant amounts of cash—loans or equity investments of up to several million dollars—entrepreneurs find it necessary to deal with sophisticated financial executives. These bankers, financiers, venture capitalists and loan officers are part of an exclusive club of men and women who really decide how, and for what, the nation's cash resources will be used. They make the decisions that influence the building of plants, hiring of employees, introduction of new products, manufacture of inventions and the marketing of a host of products and services. To these individuals, the social or scientific benefits of business ventures are of only secondary importance—the ''numbers'' are in the driver's seat. These individuals are occupied primarily with balance sheets, cash flow, income statements and the like.

This special group of people—and they are powerful people to be sure—speaks a very special language—a language all their own. It is the language of business and finance, and in its most specialized form, it is the language of leveraging.

The importance of this is made clear by the old saying, ''When in Rome do as the Romans do.'' In other words, when you are in a strange culture, you will fare best by learning and imitating the local norms and traditions. This also holds true for dealings with the financial community. Whether the entrepreneur is seeking a loan of $50,000 or an investment of $5 million, it is a real plus to approach the cash source with as much intelligence and savvy as you can muster. Financial executives are impressed by those who demonstrate command of business science including accounting, marketing and operations. And equally important, they have little confidence in those who do not know a balance sheet from a bowling score.

And how do the financial powers—those you must approach for financing—gauge an entrepreneur's level of business competence? By your resume, yes, but also by the way you speak. Those applicants who come across sounding as if they are thoroughly familiar with the business sciences will impress cash sources from the outset—and that first impression can be decisive.

SPEAKING THE LANGUAGE

In many cases, this boils down to simply knowing the terminology of business: the words, phrases and concepts commonly used in the financial community. Speak their language and the financiers will accept you as an accomplished business owner much faster than if everything they say has to be explained twice. Knowing the language of leveraging can actually help you get the money you need to start or expand your business. The terms and concepts we will review can be incorporated into your business proposal, business plan, loan application and personal interviews.

And equally important, learning the language of leveraging makes it easier to protect yourself in current and future business dealings. The better grasp you have of the other party's contracts and proposals (either written or oral), the less likely they will be able to take advantage of you by pulling the wool over your eyes. The lack of knowledge about business terms and concepts causes many entrepreneurs to fall victim to ruthless schemers. Sensing some ignorance of business language, these rip-off artists purposely use confusing jargon in order to deceive their prey. By arming yourself with a comprehensive business vocabulary, you can foil these con men. Remember, a good offense is the best defense. Learning the language of business can help you obtain more money, leverage it better and earn a greater return.

"I can tell a novice from a seasoned entrepreneur after less than five minutes of conversation," says Paul M., the chief lending officer for a major commercial bank in Duluth, Minn. "The applicant who has the kind of high-level business experience that I respect speaks as if he knows his way around a real company. I don't have to sit there and explain to him what I mean by break-even analysis or product positioning.

"The ability to talk turkey from the start, to avoid the basics and get to the heart of the matter, impresses me no end. Although I probably shouldn't say this—after all, an applicant should be judged on his overall credentials—someone who comes in here well versed in the language of business has a much better chance of getting money from me than someone who sounds uninformed. I really start making my decision before the application is formally reviewed.

"For example, I made a $300,000 loan last week to a woman who has invented a new home bathroom cleaning appliance. She's a real inventor type, no doubt about it, she lives and breathes science. Ordinarily, I would go thumbs down to that type of loan applicant because they don't make good business owners, but not this woman. She got the money, and I was on her side from the start, because she leaves her science behind when she comes in this bank: she demonstrates an in-depth understanding of business and that's what I want to know more than anything else. She speaks the language of entrepreneurship.''

A Presentation Glossary

The following glossary contains those words, terms and concepts which will prove valuable to leveraged entrepreneurs either launching or expanding their businesses. Study the definitions, learn them and use them in your business presentations.

Accounts Receivable: The sums of money owed to a business by its customers. The objective in a well-run business is to receive payment on all receivables as quickly as possible—within thirty days if possible. The longer a receivable remains outstanding, the more difficult it is to collect on it. Once payment on a receivable is made, the company's cash position increases and its receivables decrease.

Amortization Purchase: This is simply the act of purchasing something with only a percentage cash payment and then gradually paying off the rest. This type of deal, once popular with many forms of tax shelters, is still used in certain real estate transactions. Although investors may make only a small percentage down payment on the real estate, they can often deduct from taxes depreciation on the full purchase price.

Assets: Refers to that cash, securities, land, machinery, plants and the like owned by a business. The worth of a company's assets can be an important factor in collateral for loans, in purchasing insurance and in selling the venture. Entrepreneurs interested in selling their companies must make certain that the value of "hidden assets" are figured into the selling price. A tract of land, for example, purchased 10 years ago for $10,000 may be on the company's books for that amount. But in the ensuing period, development of the surrounding area or construction of a superhighway may have multiplied the value of the real estate many times over. This true value should be determined and computed into the total worth of the firm's assets.

Business Interruption Insurance: The latest innovations in business insurance can help you guard against almost every kind of risk your venture faces. Whether the threat is from natural disasters, credit losses or human error, policies can be written to cover your potential losses. The objective is to find the ideal combination of adequate coverage and manageable premiums. Investors and lenders alike are sticklers for good insurance protection: they want to make certain that top managers, physical assets and business volume have as much insurance protection as possible.

One of the best types of little-known policies that investors like to see is Business Interruption Insurance. Indirect losses resulting from a fire or similar disaster can be as costly as the actual physical damage. Closing down operations for rebuilding, for example, can cause severe financial pressures. Continuing expenses such as salaries and taxes must be paid, even though new sales are not being made. Business Interruption Insurance helps you cope with those difficult times by paying the amounts of profits and revenues your firm would normally earn. Since the duration of the payments depends on the policy terms, you must work with your agent to project a realistic recovery period.

Backlog: This rather obscure but highly-useful indicator measures the amount of future sales already committed to a business. For example, let's say a home building company is currently working on 10 homes worth $1 million but has deposits on the books for another five homes it will start to construct in six months. If those future homes will sell for $100,000 each, the builder has a backlog of $500,000. This is a significant measurement because it informs management of its minimum level of future volume and helps prepare for the purchasing of raw materials, hiring labor and arranging loans.

Business Brokers: Are specialists in arranging the sale and purchases of businesses. Let's say that as part of your long-term leveraged strategy, you want to sell one business and purchase another. In many cases, the use of brokers to handle these transactions is the most productive approach. Brokers know the ropes and they are the people best equipped to move the company to sale quickly and profitably. You will, however, have to pay for this expertise: Brokers retain ten percent or more of the selling price as commission.

Still, the brokerage fee is often a worthy investment. Brokers earn their fees by tapping a wide network of business contacts, assessing and screening potential buyers and negotiating a valid

contract suitable to both parties. In short, brokers boost the chances
of selling the business and then reduce the red tape in the ensuing
transactions. Bankers, attorneys and accountants can usually
recommend the names of qualified brokers.

Commercial Appraisals: Once you've built your business into a
going concern, it's only natural to want to know how much it is worth.
What price would it fetch on the open market? How much does it add
to your personal wealth?

Surprisingly enough, very few entrepreneurs really know the
answers. They know what their business means to them in personal
terms but not what it represents in dollars and cents. Although this
personal factor is important to the individual, it has no impact on
lenders or investors. These cash sources want to know what the company is worth in hard figures—not in terms of the owner's ego or self
esteem. To succeed as a leveraged entrepreneur, you'll have to give
them what they want.

Commercial appraisers can help. These consultants are experts
at gauging the value of privately-held companies. In return for a
specified fee, appraisers will launch a full-scale evaluation of your
business, putting a price tag on everything from fixed assets to good
will (the value of a firm's reputation). You'll know what your company is worth to everyone from the insurance inspector to the big
conglomerate looking to buy you out.

Appraisals take about 30 days from start to finish and may cost
from $2000 to $3000. One appraisal may, however, be designed for a
number of purposes, including insurance claims, tax reviews and
loan applications. Bankers and accountants can recommend the
names of reputable appraisers.

Commercial Factoring: This service aids a company's cash
flow by advancing cash payments on the basis of accounts
receivable. Factoring goes to the heart of the problem of late payment, enabling you as a business manager to collect up front on all
sums owed to your firm. Rather than waiting out slow paying
accounts, you simply send all sales invoices directly to a factor, who
immediately reimburses you for up to 80 percent of invoice values.
Factors assume the worry and expense of late payments. As part of
their total service package, they also prepare sales ledgers, implement and maintain credit controls and manage your collection
program. This protection further strengthens your cash flow and is

particularly valuable for overseas transactions where customer credit standings are often questionable. For small firms, factoring's key benefit is the assurance of available funds. Once sales have been made, cash is available for a large percentage of your receipts. For this service, factors generally charge the bank overdraft rate for all advances as well as an additional service fee.

Clifford Trusts: As a leveraged entrepreneur, you will want to protect as much of your earnings from the tax man as you legally can. This means ferreting out little-known, yet highly attractive, financial devices. One such device is the Clifford Trust. This arrangement enables entrepreneurs to cut the costs of their children's college by 50 percent or more. The procedure works as follows: the income from specially-designed trusts is directed to the children, thus reducing taxes on the income. In many cases, the savings are adequate to cover a substantial percentage of tuition costs. Get the details from your accountant.

Debenture: This is an unsecured bond issued by a corporation which is backed only by the credit standing of the issuer. It can be an excellent way for sound firms to raise substantial sums.

Demographics: Are profiles of groups of people identifying their characteristics, including age, sex, income levels and the like. For business purposes, demographics are used to study the composition of various markets to determine the types of consumers in it. The demographics of a particular community or region are important, for example, when an entrepreneur is considering launching a chain of stores. Let's say it is record shops that you have in mind. In order to get the funds to start your venture, you'll likely have to prove to investors that the demographics of the area will support record stores. In this case, the studies should reveal a high concentration of young and affluent consumers in the area. These are the people who buy the great bulk of the records sold in this country.

Depreciation: This is basically an accounting term which refers to the allowance made for a loss in value because of wear, age or other cause. In operating a business, depreciation allowances on the company's assets can be vital for tax purposes.

Direct Marketing: This increasingly popular alternative to traditional sales techniques can help companies tap new markets without investing substantial capital in stores, plants or equipment The concept is simple. By eliminating the middleman, direct marketing slashes many of the costs involved in launching new products or services. Direct marketers cut out wholesale and retail distributors and sell directly to consumers through the mails or with advertising. The strategy enables merchants and manufacturers to test expansion ideas on a shoestring. There is no need to build stores or to hire sales representatives. Most plans can be tried out for the cost of an ad or two and some postage. Additional investments can be made after the concept proves out, thus eliminating the usual gamble.

What's more, direct marketing seems to be an approach geared to the temper of the times. Recent statistics indicate that direct sales are rising, exceeding $60 billion per year. Convenience and savings are the key attractions. The best way to get started in a direct marketing effort is to work with an agency specializing in this field. For recommendations, and additional information, contact the Direct Selling Association, 1730 M Street, N.W., Washington, D.C. 20036. (202-293-5760).

Equating Velocities: The proper pricing of your products or services is one of those business functions that often gets brushed over by novice entrepreneurs. Selling prices are too frequently based on intuition or on manufacturers' suggestions. Neither one of these approaches is adequate. One excellent way to adjust your pricing is by a technique called Equating Velocities.

Let's say you are entertaining the idea of reducing your markup per item in order to draw more customers. When to take this step and how far you can go can be figured through equating velocities, which works according to the following formula: If your business is operating on a 33-percent gross margin and you are thinking of reducing this to 30 percent in order to lure customers from the competition, you must first determine the amount of increased sales volume you'll need to yield, in dollars, a gross margin at least as large as you now earn.

To get the answer, divide the present markup percentage by the lower figure under consideration: 33 percent divided by 30 equals 1.10. Thus for every dollar of present volume, 1.10 or 10 percent more in sales will be needed to compensate for the lower markup. If you are relatively sure that the lower markup will boost sales considerably more than 10 percent, then the cut in markup is a sound business move. It will result in greater profits for your business.

Employee Stock Ownership Plans (ESOPs): These financial devices are similar to employee compensation programs such as profit sharing, but with a major difference. Instead of cash benefits, Employee Stock Ownership Plans are used to offer employees part ownership in the firm through stock bonus awards. Aside from the employee relations benefits of ESOPs, however, there is the additional advantage of being able to use them to raise capital at lower than the usual costs. Let's say, for example, that you need a new office facility. Providing your credit rating is good, you can likely get a construction loan from a bank. The total amount will be financed over several years and the interest payments are deductible.

With ESOPs, however, you can go a step further: you can deduct the full amount of the loan—interest and principle. The extra tax deduction helps to bring down the cost of borrowing. The procedure works as follows: management arranges for a bank loan to be made directly to the ESOP. As head of the company, you guarantee the loan and agree to repay it with annual contributions to the plan. Since the plan's contributions are tax deductible, you can deduct the full amount of the loan. This can yield savings of up to 50 percent compared to traditional financing terms. Check with your accountant for details.

Export Management Companies: Expert assistance in moving products to overseas markets is available from private as well as governmental outfits. Since investors may want your company to tap as many markets as possible, knowing how to reach overseas is crucial. Specialized consulting firms will help you plan and implement complete export programs. Known as Export Management Companies(EMC), these consultants have practical experience in all facets of foreign trade. They function as your right hand, working closely with clients throughout the course of their overseas activities.

Success in working with EMCs depends, to a great extent, on the selection of the consultant best suited to meet your needs. The field is wide and diverse: from 600 to 1000 EMCs operate in the U.S., ranging in size from single consultants to major professional firms employing hundreds of trade experts. Help in making the right choice is available from the Federation of Export Management Companies, PO Box 7612, Washington, D.C. 20044.

Once you have made a selection, the EMC assumes all export functions. Most prefer to work on a fee basis, buying products from you at a discount and selling them overseas for a profit. The discount is open to negotiation but generally falls slightly below wholesale. Remember, working with EMCs can give you access to many international markets and this can be impressive to potential investors and lenders. Even if your volume of business abroad is not big, the prestige of selling there can go a long way in terms of attracting eager investors.

Horizontal Expansion: For the purposes of leveraged entrepreneurs, this concept refers to buying out the competition. It is a means of propelling a company to rapid and dramatic growth by simply purchasing existing ventures in the field. A small dry cleaning chain, for example, can quickly double its size through horizontal expansion by buying out other dry cleaning shops. Many investors prefer to fund this type of expansion, rather than the starting of new businesses by scratch, because horizontal expansion enables them to deal with known quantities. The shops being purchased are going ventures with established track records. The element of risk is therefore reduced. Consider this type of expansion as one of the ways to attract lenders and investors.

Integrated Business: Some companies, like the giant oil firms, are fully integrated in that they account for their own production, distribution and marketing. They take raw products, refine them, transport them to distribution centers and even market them. Integration is an enviable condition, because it enables management to control many of the factors affecting the business (including supply prices), and because it generally allows for greater profit margins. Leveraged entrepreneurs seeking substantial growth companies may want to aim for integration by gradually buying out their own suppliers, wholesalers and the like.

Leasing: Expansion-minded entrepreneurs can use leasing to acquire needed business assets. This increasingly popular alternative to traditional ownership of assets let's you utilize commercial equipment without making major capital investments. It is a way to pay as you grow, thereby conserving cash for more pressing needs.

The economics of leasing are especially attractive to small firms. Rather than setting aside substantial sums of money for down payments or for outright purchases, leasing let's you make manageable monthly or annual payments. Leasing also serves as a hedge against inflation. By signing a long-term lease you are assured of stable rates regardless of inflationary pressures. And, by not investing present cash reserves in equipment purchases, it is possible to make future lease payments with deflated dollars.

Most importantly, you can obtain complete financing of equipment costs on terms tailored to your company's special needs. As a rule, leasing offers a more flexible financing than do banks or other lending institutions. A wide range of business assets can now be leased—everything from company cars to office buildings to computers. Check the yellow pages for leasing companies or look to your own commercial bank. A good number of banks now offer business leases through their subsidiaries.

Letter of Credit: Those firms which do venture into the foreign markets must be familiar with the so called "letter of credit." This is a frequently-used form of collection in export transactions. The credit document, issued by a bank at the buyer's request, promises to pay the seller a specified sum of money upon receipt of cargo delivery papers. Although letters of credit may be revocable or irrevocable, the exporter should insist on the latter. This means that once credit has been accepted by the seller, it can not be altered in any way by the buyer.

Small exporters must minimize risk conditions, so the owner-manager should insist that the letter of credit be confirmed through a U.S. bank, which makes it responsible for payment regardless of the financial condition of the buyer or the foreign bank. Additional information on export payment forms may be obtained from international banking departments or from any U.S. Department of Commerce District Office.

Limited Partnerships: Choosing the right form of business organization can have a major impact on a company's ability to raise funds. Although many entrepreneurs are not aware of this, there are alternatives to the three most common forms of organization: partnership, proprietorship and corporation. One key option is the limited partnership. This offers some of the benefits of both partnerships and corporations. Here, investors in the business can become partners in it without assuming unlimited liability. The advantage of this form is that you may use it to attract investors unwilling to risk personal liability. It is important to be aware, however, that limited partnerships tend to come under closer IRS scrutiny than general partnerships. That is because many questionable tax shelter plans which have surfaced in recent years have taken the form of limited partnerships.

Liquidity: This is a rather complex matter from an accounting standpoint, but for our purposes here it can be boiled down to a simple definition: Liquidity is the ability to pay your bills. It answers the question, "Do I have enough cash, plus assets that can be readily turned into cash, to pay all the debts that will come due this accounting period?"

Failure to keep your company sufficiently liquid means you cannot pay your bills. It is the best way to "back yourself into a corner" to permanently damage your business and, perhaps most important for leveraged entrepreneurs, it can produce a stain on your reputation that will discourage investors and lenders from working with you. It can have the same stigma that personal bankruptcy leaves on individuals—just try to get credit once you have been declared bankrupt.

For ways to test and monitor your liquidity, check this glossary under "Ratios."

Market Segments: One of the hallmarks of modern marketing is the movement away from the old shotgun approach towards reaching customers and increasing reliance on expert marksmanship. What this means is that the most sophisticated business managers operating today carefully isolate those groups of customers most likely to buy their goods or services. Only after these groups—or market segments—have been identified, do the owners launch their promotional and sales activities.

The reason is clear. Knowing precisely who you are selling to saves time and money on misdirected marketing efforts. Let's say you are producing a line of trendy sportswear. Research shows you that the market segment most likely to purchase your apparel is composed of middle class, urban, teenage girls ages 14 to 18. By knowing your primary segment, you can limit advertising to rock music stations and teen fashion magazines. You know not to waste money on 4-H Club publications because rural consumers are not attracted to your goods.

By definition, market segments are those groups of consumers who share similar tastes, preferences or purchasing habits. Demonstrate your skills in segmenting markets and you will most likely impress entrepreneurs with your expertise.

Money Market Funds: Simply obtaining funds is not the only important consideration for leveraged entrepreneurs. It is also wise to make maximum use of those funds while they are sitting idle, waiting to be invested in the business. One good way to turn idle cash into extra profits is to dabble in the nation's money market funds.

Once the exclusive domain of corporate giants, money market transactions are now practical for the little guy as well. Rather than face the market head-on, small firms should limit their dealings to money market funds. This approach enables inexperienced managers to obtain the benefits of money market transactions at limited risk.

Money market funds buy and sell investment vehicles such as government securities, commercial paper and certificates of deposit. The goal is to earn profits for both the fund and its investors. Here's how it works: Let's say a small contractor receives a lump sum payment of $47,000, half of which must be paid to suppliers in 20 days. Rather than letting the money sit idle in a company checking account until payment is made, management can put the cash to work in a money market fund. That way the money will earn interest from the day of deposit to the day of withdrawal.

Entrepreneurs can use money market funds as "cash parking lots." The dividend rates are comparable with bank interest rates (although this is subject to change according to prevailing conditions), but the funds pay out every day the money is invested with them—there is no penalty for early withdrawals. Among the major money market funds worth exploring are Merrill Lynch's Ready Asset Fund and the Dreyfus Liquid Asset Fund.

Multiple Write-offs: This refers to those tax shelters which enable individuals to write off several times the amount they invest in a business deal. In a typical multiple write off, a $25,000 investment could yield a whopping tax write off of up to $100,000. Many investors participating in these shelters are not really concerned whether or not the investment itself turns out to be profitable: the multiple write off alone is sufficient to make the deal very attractive, especially to high-bracket earners.

The bad news is that the IRS has cracked down hard on multiple write offs, leaving only a few variations still standing, mostly in real estate. The best way to take advantage of the most productive deals is to make contact with a sharp accountant or tax attorney who can put you into the shelters.

Positioning: Another of the key principles of modern marketing is known as "positioning." This concept stems from the recognition that no product or service can be all things to all people—that in this age of specialization, even products and services should stake a claim to some special appeal or performance factor. This relates closely to the market segmentation phenomenon: certain groups of consumers have similar tastes, preferences and buying habits. By positioning a product to appeal to these segments, you can improve the chances for its success.

A classic case of positioning is Marlboro cigarettes. First introduced as a woman's smoke, it had feminine-looking ads and a very subtle approach. When the brand failed to sell well, its maker, Philip Morris, decided to "reposition" it to appeal to men. Thus, the macho Marlboro Man campaign emerged and has taken the brand to the top position in its industry—the number one cigarette in the U.S.

Rather than trying to appeal to all smokers, Marlboro's positioning focused on those market segments that would be attracted to a manly, outdoor image. The positioning strategy can be applied to any business, no matter how small. Even a local dress shop, for example, must decide whether it will aim for mass appeal, wealthy matrons or young teens. The right positioning can add much to its success. When making a proposal to investors, the positioning strategy should always be included.

Profit Analysis: Good management means using certain computations to monitor operating results. There are a number of basic formulas you can apply—simple enough to do without professional assistance—that can help you identify trends in the making. To conduct a profit analysis, as this is often called, you should first determine your gross profit by subtracting the cost of goods sold (those costs related to obtaining and producing goods held for sale) from net sales (total sales minus returns and allowances.) Frequently computing this key business indicator is an excellent way to monitor sudden changes or long-term trends in operating performance. A steep drop in gross profits may, for example, signal deep-seated problems. Variances in gross profit from one accounting period to another may be due to changes in sales caused by changes in selling price (sales-price variance) or changes in volume of goods sold (sales-volume variance) or they may be related to the cost of goods sold caused by changes in unit price (cost-price variance) or by changes in volume of goods sold (cost-volume variance).

Your profit analysis computations should be considered part of the tools of the trade of the sophisticated leveraged entrepreneur.

Proprietorship: The sole proprietorship is the form of business organization generally recommended for starting a small business, because it is easy to launch and rather simple to terminate.

Extremely flexible, proprietorships are suitable for firms involved in virtually every type of business function. Proprietorships do not require government approval, profits are taxed as part of the owner's personal income and the sole owner is personally liable for all of the company's debts and taxes. In addition, startup costs are very low for the proprietorship form. Fees are payable only for licensing (where applicable) and registration. Total cost is often under $100.

The financial risk to the owner is, however, greatest under the proprietorship form. In the event that existing assets are insufficient to satisfy creditor claims, the proprietor is liable for all debts of the business—liable to the extent of his or her personal property. For this reason, I advise against using the proprietorship form for highly-leveraged ventures. Since the risks of collapse with this type of venture are great, the entrepreneur must do as much as possible to protect his personal assets—to limit liability.

Turn-Around Situations: Frequently, for one reason or another, business ventures go on the skids. This happens both to established companies and to newly-launched firms: Suddenly all seems to be going wrong, sales and profits are declining and there seems to be no hope in sight.

Strange as it may seem, there are some business managers who thrive on entering the scene at this point and who are expert at making these seemingly hopeless ventures into "turn-around situations." This means that the business is put back on its feet financially and is restored to a healthy growth pattern.

Turn-around experts do their magic by paring off losing subsidiaries, dropping unprofitable products, closing unproductive stores, slashing the payroll, stepping up promotional activities or any combination of these and other actions. The point is that they are able to make winners and cut losers, and this earns them almost heroic status with the business and financial community. Any evidence of an entrepreneur's ability to direct turn-around situations should be called to the attention of potential lenders and investors. It can be an excellent way to build confidence in your abilities and free up substantial amounts of needed capital.

Ratios: Two of the most reliable ratios for testing the liquidity of a business are as follows:

Current Ratio is computed from the balance sheet by dividing current assets by current liabilities. For example, ABC Manufacturing, with current assets of $140,000 and current liabilities of $60,000, has a current ratio of 2.3 to 1.

$$\frac{\text{current assets} = \$140,000}{\text{current liabilities} = \$60,000} = 2.3$$

A ratio of two to one or better is deemed sufficient to keep the company solvent even in times of minor setbacks. This is traditional thinking, however. As a leveraged entrepreneur, you may dip below the 2 to 1 ratio.

Acid-Test Ratio is more exacting than the current ratio. By not including inventories, it focuses on liquid assets:

$$\frac{\text{cash} + \text{government securities} + \text{receivables}}{\text{current liabilities}}$$

For ABC Manufacturing, which has no government securities, this becomes $70,000 divided by $60,000, resulting in an acid-test ratio of 1.2 to 1. An acid-test ratio of one to one is considered satisfactory.

Trade Secrets: One of the best ways to attract big-league financing is to make investors "an offer they can't refuse." Meaning? Offer them something with such assurance of success that they are actually afraid of losing out on something big.

This frequently occurs when the entrepreneur seeking funds is armed with a promising patent. But the patent process is long, complex and costly, taking several years and many thousands of dollars to culminate. One little-known alternative to patents, known as trade secrets, can be equally effective for use in obtaining funds and in protecting unique business assets.

Trade secrets are exactly what the name implies: business information that must remain secret to be effective. To qualify as a trade secret, the information must lend a competitive advantage, must be kept secret within your company and must not be generally known within your field or industry.

Examples of common types of trade secrets are:

1. Processes you develop for manufacturing foodstuffs, components or industrial materials

2. Formulas for manufacturing dyes, compounds or cosmetic products

3. Techniques for producing equipment

Trade secrets meeting all established criteria are protected from competitive infringement. The Supreme Court's landmark ruling declaring trade secrets independent of the federal patent system saw to that. What this means to you is the freedom to choose between patents and trade secrets.

The major drawback to trade secrets is that they are vulnerable to independent development. Competitors may duplicate secret processes by experimenting on their own. Since legal restraints apply only to copying or stealing data on which trade secrets are based, competitors are free to develop imitations based on their own research. Still, the chances of them coming up with your unique idea are slim. What's more, you can use trade secrets to interest investors and then go for the formal patent procedure once you have the money in hand.

Umbrella Policies: Leveraged finance carries a good deal of risk—there's no doubt about it. With this in mind, those entrepreneurs best at leveraging do all within their power to limit the risks without impeding their company's growth. One way to do this is with insurance. It is the last category you should check on your leveraged checklist before getting started with the actual business venture.

Keep in mind that spiraling inflation and ever-higher jury awards have combined to swell liability settlements to record levels. One freak business accident can jeopardize all personal assets. Years of business gains can be lost in a single law suit. The solution is clear: highly vulnerable individuals must step up insurance protection to maximum levels. Supplemental liability coverage, designed to cover risks excluded by other policies, is the first step. These so-called "umbrella policies" offer up to $1 million protection for little more than $100 per year. Check with your insurance broker or with any of the major property and casualty insurance outfits.

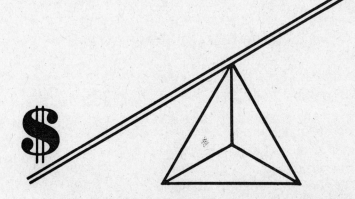

ASSETS, BALANCE SHEETS
AND THE IMPORTANCE
OF PROJECTING
FINANCIAL STRENGTH

Throughout the career of a leveraged entrepreneur, two factors remain constant; the search for additional funds and the need to maintain an aura of financial strength and stability. Both of these key elements of leveraging are closely-related.

Let's take a closer look at this relationship. We say that the search for additional funds is constant because most leveraged entrepreneurs are the types of individuals who are simply not satisfied with marginal success. If they start a new venture, all goes well and it is profitable from the start, the leveraged entrepreneur only sees this as a stepping stone to establishing a really substantial business operation. Limited success is rarely the final objective.

The same is true of the established business owner who turns to leveraging for expansion purposes. Take the woman who has owned two growing and profitable hair salons for 15 years and suddenly recognizes that through leveraging she can hope to own 50 salons. Since she is the kind of agressive individual who is willing to embark on the strategy of leveraging at midpoint in her life—willing to tackle an entirely new business concept—then she is not likely to be satisfied once her chain of salons totals 50. If she's typical of gutsy and ambitious (some say driven) leveraged business owners, she will set her sights on 100 shops as soon as she has accumulated 25. Once successful entrepreneurs get a taste of the mechanics of leveraging—and it works for them—they can never get enough. They want wealth, power and all of the things that lead to business success on a grand scale.

So, this voracious appetite for business expansion activates a tremendous demand for additional cash to grow the business. Borrowed cash, invested cash, lines of credit—you name it and the leveraged entrepreneur continues to seek it out constantly—in many cases even after retirement (see Chapter 11). As that hair salon, restaurant or gas station chain—or that manufacturing firm or service outfit—continues its dynamic expansion, it will need more stores, plants, personnel, equipment, advertising, legal services, raw materials, patents, vehicles and the like. And that shopping list will require copious amounts of cash or carte blanche credit.

Keeping this financing flowing is the owner-manager's responsibility—and the best way to be successful at it is to maintain the company's appearance of strength. Here, we can borrow a page from the great diplomats of the world: Churchill, Roosevelt and Kissinger all strove to negotiate from a position of strength. They always knew that any requests or demands made of other parties were much more effective if power was behind the plea, rather than fear or weakness. Believe it or not, the same is true when approaching loan sources. As we have said, the best way to get financing is to appear as if you don't need it. Complain that your venture will collapse without the money and you'll get pity but not a cent of capital.

As the entrepreneur moves into the big leagues and ever-larger sums of capital are required, this aura of strength becomes even more important. Once the business is seeking financing in the million-dollar-plus category, you will have to be certain to impress lenders with your strength—with your ability to repay the loan or return healthy dividends on the investment. In addition to these purely financial considerations, everyone likes to go with a winner. Appear as if you are headed for the top and you will find that many cash sources want to hang onto your coattails and go along for the ride. It's the same as politics—the top candidates get all the money, all the volunteers and all the press coverage that they need.

HOW ONE MAN USED
PROJECTED FINANCIAL STRENGTH

"There are two ways to develop that aura of strength—of being a winner," says Myron E., owner of a thriving boat-making business that produces custom luxury yachts for some of the nation's wealthiest families. Myron's Aqua Alpha Industries is at the top of his field now—but it wasn't always that way. Starting off with $535 of his own and an idea for a unique type of inflatable raft, Myron was, at first, too poor to put his invention into production—too poor to even patent it. Instead of wringing his hands and worrying about his predicament, however, Myron knew just what to do to change his financial status rather quickly. Armed with sketches and a small model of his raft, he approached the sporting goods buyer for Macy's to test that company's interest in his invention. Well, it was love at first sight. The buyer expressed great enthusiasm for the raft and promised a huge order should the final product turn out according to plan.

That was all Myron had to hear. The very next day, he ordered an advertisement in the "Capital Wanted" section of the Wall Street Journal, stating the following:

Talented inventor with exclusive plans for dynamic new consumer product in the rapidly-growing leisure field seeks silent partner to provide $1 million for production and marketing. Product has initial support of major national department store. Offers only from well-funded investors willing to remain completely silent will be entertained.

Myron's ad accomplished a number of key things. First, it established the fact that this was a unique and novel product in a growth industry. Since investors tend to follow fads—they all like to be a part of the latest hot industry—calling attention to your industry if it is one currently in vogue makes good sense. In recent years, high technology, anti-pollution and leisure products have enjoyed this special status.

The ad also made it clear that the product was more than just some wild inventor's crazy pipe dream. By mentioning the support of a major national department store, Myron assured investors that this was no naive scientist looking for funds—but was instead a practical businessman who has a clear understanding of commercial necessities. All too many inventors never consider the commercial applications of their work. They just invent for invention's sake—and that's something the investment community wants no part of.

By lining up sales interest even before the product was patented, Myron dispelled any notion of his lack of business sense.

And, perhaps most important, Myron's ad took a tough stance. By stressing his minimum requirements—and by laying down the law on the kind of partner he required—Myron was taking that all-important position of strength. The illusion that he was in the catbird seat—that he could call the shots—was enough to build the kind of investor stampede other inventors just dream about. As a result, Myron's post office box at New York's Grand Central Post Office was blessed with twelve serious offers for substantial financing the same week the ad ran.

After a dozen interviews, Myron decided to work with Kristen R., a wealthy widow looking for a way to parlay her already substantial life insurance proceeds. She proved to be a perfect match for Myron's needs: Kristin had no business acumen and did not pretend anything to the contrary. She had substantial funds to invest and just wanted to lean back and see her money grow. She paid for Myron's patent, hired him a top-notch attorney and marketing vice president, and funded the firm until it had its first order of rafts on the market. To this day, she does not know just how desperate Myron was when he first met her.

Once the funds were in his corner, success came quickly to Myron. His rafts were advertised nationally, were sold in Macy's, Sears, K-Mart, Korvettes, Caldor, Herman's and in thousands of sporting goods shops. In three years, he was generating revenues of

$9 million and drawing an annual salary of $125,000 plus a company Cadillac, ski lodge and a long list of perks.

Enough for Myron? Enough for a man who'd spent his previous 20 working years as a door-to-door salesman and gadget tinkerer earning less than $18,000 a year? "Not nearly enough," says Myron himself. "When I realized how far I had come on borrowed funds, I wanted to go even further. Oh, I know all of the sayings about being greedy and the like but I wanted to own an enormous home, a villa in France, antique cars—the whole shooting match."

Myron's strategy for doing this was to graduate to yachts—no steps in between. Right from rafts to yachts. Knowing his limitations as a yacht designer, he hired a promising and talented young naval architect, gave him $100,000 and eight months to develop some highly-unusual designs, used some raft profits to build a prototype model of his Aqua Alpha Luxury Cruiser Yacht and then went after bank financing of $7 million to get the firm on-stream as a major boatworks.

"Just as I had done when lining up the money for the rafts, I approached the banks from a position of strength. First, I hired a public relations agency to put together a slick financial presentation clearly establishing my credentials as a business owner and inventor, my astounding track record with the rafts and, most important, the solid financial position my firm already enjoyed. We wanted the bankers to know that they were dealing with a sound manager and a solid company.

"To add the crowning touch, however, I brought along my ace in the hole. Just as I had used the Macy's interest to sell the raft idea, I made sure to presell a very well known local industrialist on purchasing one of my Aqua Alpha Yachts and secured his commitment to buy in advance of full production. Not only that, but the gentlemen, who is an expert boatsman and commodore of a prestigious New York yacht club, agreed to come along with me to the bank meeting. He loved quality boats and truly wanted to see my venture succeed. His presence at the meeting, held on a bright sunny morning on Wall Street, all but sewed up the deal and got me my money on the first go round. An influential customer and a sophisticated financial presentation combined to overwhelm the bankers and I was on my way again."

There are important lessons to be learned from Myron's successful borrowing techniques. Not just in the use of prestigious customer commitments but also in the mechanics of his financial presentations. One of the most important aspects here is the balance sheet. This is crucial for established firms seeking to expand and for newly-launched or startup firms (in the latter case, projected balance sheets will have to be prepared.) Balance sheets can be used to build that all-important image of financial strength. Let's take a closer look at balance sheets.

BALANCE SHEETS

The balance sheet is a report on the financial condition of a business at a particular date in time. It reveals the firm's assets, its liabilities and the owner's equity. The following is an example of a simple balance sheet:

ABC CORPORATION
BALANCE SHEET
FEBRUARY 12, 1965

ASSETS		LIABILITIES AND STOCKHOLDERS' EQUITY	
Cash	$2,795.00	Liabilities:	
Accounts Receivable	1,250.00	Accounts Payable	$1,200.00
Component Parts	3,800.00	Stockholders' Equity:	
Real Estate	1,500.00	Capital Stock	$8,000.00
		Retained Earnings	145.00
	$9,345.00		$9,345.00

Since ABC is a corporation, the owner's equity is referred to as "stockholders' equity": That is because the stockholders are the owners of a corporation. If this were a partnership or proprietorship, ownership could be expressed on the balance sheet as partners' or proprietor's equity respectively.

The elements that make up the balance sheet include the "assets," which are the things of value owned by the firm. Here, we have cash balances (which tend to be low in leveraged firms), accounts receivable, physical plant, real estate, machinery and even patents. This last item is extremely important for leveraged entrepreneurs. Since your firms will tend to be short on cash reserves, building up the extent of non-cash assets, especially intangibles, can help to project that aura of financial strength. Intangibles include patents, trademarks, trade names and goodwill. These are considered assets because they offer certain rights and services to the owner.

"We had a very well-respected firm of commercial appraisers put a price tag on the worth of the patents I secured for my novel yacht designs," Myron notes. "Our design features assured fast-moving boats that were also extremely sea worthy and comfortable. This powerful combination of features would make the boats highly desirable, from a market standpoint, and that's why the appraisers put a very substantial price tag on the value of the patents. Of course, this figure moved on to the left column of our balance sheet and gave the impression of substantial financial strength—just the thing investors look for."

For established businesses, the value of good will or trade names should never be overlooked. A trade name which commands consumer loyalty is certainly a valuable asset and one which lenders and investors appreciate for its commercial value. There's no denying that the very famous trade names—Coca-Cola, Pepsi, Kleenex, Crest—play a major part in their owners' business success. Big companies such as Coca-Cola have staffs of individuals whose sole responsibility it is to safeguard and protect the firm's trademark against misuse or duplication. Although your business trademark may not be as well-known as Coke's, it can be significant in your market area or industry and should therefore be listed among the firm's assets.

Good will refers to the positive market acceptance the company has built up over the years. Again, this is an intangible asset with considerable value to many firms. The manufacturer of industrial equipment that has produced quality products for a decade or more, supported its guarantees, met delivery schedules, credited damaged or defective goods, satisfied customer requests even when extra efforts were required and kept its prices reasonable, has generated good will throughout its industry. What this means is that customers trust it, like doing business with it and will continue to patronize it.

This, too, is what investors look for when reviewing business ventures.

The liabilities column of the balance sheet refers to the debts of the business. These are the amounts owed to the company's creditors. Included here are accounts payable, which are the invoices for goods and services that have been purchased on open account, mortgages and notes payable. Liabilities are often categorized as current or long-term. Generally speaking, the former refers to those liabilities which are to be paid within one year of the date of the balance sheet and the latter to those due after one year. Accounts payable are almost always current liabilities; mortgages payable are usually long-term liabilities.

The owner's equity in the company is computed by subtracting the liabilities from the sum of the assets. Thus, a business with assets of $10,300,000 and liabilities of $5,300,000, has an owners' equity of $5,000,000. A substantial owners' equity is considered a strong plus in obtaining additional funds.

The balance sheet should be viewed as more than a simple instrument for impressing potential lenders and investors. It can also be used to provide the entrepreneur with crucial information on how to direct his business. For example, preparation of the balance sheet may reveal to the owner that the company already has too much long-term debt and that additional funds should be secured through short-term borrowing or through equity infusions.

Balance sheets can also be helpful for discovering potential trouble spots. A review of balance sheets for the preceding five years may reveal that more and more of the firm's assets are under the category of inventory. This may indicate a slow and unhealthy buildup of excess inventories—too much of the corporation's cash may be invested in the back room. Further investigations of the matter will be required.

"It is always a good idea for business owners to be somewhat familiar with the mechanics and the meaning of balance sheets," says Dale M., a certified public accountant from Louisville, Ky. "All of the major financial reports serve as barometers of what is happening within the company—where it stands now, where it is in relation to the past and where it seems to be heading. It is especially important for the leveraged entrepreneur to know these kinds of things—to be up to the minute on all aspects of his operations—because his is such a fast-moving and volatile type of venture."

There is no doubt that the preparation and analysis of balance sheets, income statements and related reports should be handled by experienced accountants. The owners should be familiar with these forms so that they can give some advice and then their consent, but the nuts and bolts technical work should be left to the experts.

SELECTING AN ACCOUNTANT

For this reason, the selection of a good accountant is an important procedure for the leveraged entrepreneur. But, like Alice in Wonderland, the business owner in search of professional services enters a bewildering world of strange terms and exotic characters. In most cases, confusion is the order of the day.

Nowhere is the problem greater than in the razzle-dazzle world of business finance. Round after round of new tax codes, investment laws and legal rulings have combined to form a complex maze of financial regulations which are far above the head of the average layman. As a result, even the language of modern finance is virtually incomprehensible to all but the experts. Only the specialists can decipher their own jargon.

The solution, then, is to rely on financial professionals. For small business owners and managers, this means hiring private accountants to handle the firm's finances. Although there are substantial fees involved, the investment is considered essential to running a leveraged business venture.

The problem is, how can the self-employed select competent accountants? How can small merchants and manufacturers make rational decisions about a field they find complex and confusing? How can entrepreneurs determine if one accountant or another is better equipped to handle small business interests?

"Choosing a certified public accountant (CPA) does not have to be a haphazard procedure," says a spokesman for the American Institute of Certified Public Accountants (AICPA). "There are ways to make an intelligent decision without being an expert in the field. The business owner must, however, be willing to devote considerable time and effort to a thorough review of the alternatives."

Experts from the AICPA—the national organization representing 130,000 CPAs—recommend the following guidelines for starting and maintaining productive accountant-client relationships:

1. Contact your state accounting society (listed in the white pages) for the names of three or four CPAs in your area. Set up exploratory sessions to determine the level of expertise each practitioner has in your specific field of business. Also, use this time to review likely fee schedules and recommended services.

2. Before making a selection, touch bases with the accountant's existing clients. Feel free to ask blunt questions about the CPA's track record, work style and accessibility.

   "If the CPA has some experience in your type of business—and his work is respected by present clients—then the odds are good that you will find a sure match with this practitioner," the AICPA spokesman adds, "Any concern about the individual's accreditation should be soothed by knowing that every CPA is fully accredited by the state in which he practices. To earn and retain the CPA title, the practitioner must pass an initial licensing exam and must usually engage in continuing education."

3. In selecting between an accounting firm or an individual CPA, be aware that firms generally offer a wider range of expertise in accounting functions. The same firm, for example, may boast partners specializing in estates, taxes and auditing. Sole practitioners, on the other hand, often charge less and provide greater individual attention.

4. Keep in mind that in firms with CPA in the title, every partner must be a certified public accountant—those below the level of partner need not, however, be CPAs. When dealing with accounting firms, stress your preference for working with partners only.

5. If your firm requires a highly-specialized practitioner, in retailing, manufacturing or service industries, ask your banker or trade association for the names of CPAs experienced in this kind of work. When your company has special needs, it is best to work with accountants well versed in the function rather than those who must "learn on the job."

6. Most accountants base their fees on the amount of time required to service the client. Determine, in advance, if your company's needs are great enough to warrant hiring the CPA on an annual retainer rather than a per-project basis. For those small firms with substantial accounting requirements, the retainer system may prove most economical and effective in the long run.

"When it comes to projecting the financial strength and stability of a client firm, a good, savvy accountant can really earn his fee," adds Dale M. "Although I am a firm believer in staying completely within the law and within accepted accounting procedures, there are ways of presenting a company to potential investors so that the cash required for growth is very likely to be forthcoming.

"One of my clients is a very highly leveraged beverage distributor and retailer that now employs 212 people and generates revenues of $16 million per year. I'm safe in saying that virtually all of this was built on borrowed funds even though the president, Abe. L., first came to me when he had little more than a dream, a few dollars and a vision for success. By packaging his plans and assets in the best possible way, we've been able to woo bankers, government lending officers and silent partners to pony up the cash Abe has needed over the years. He's grown quite prosperous because of this."

To sum it all up, I suggest that leveraged entrepreneurs know their way around financial reports. No matter how smart your accountant is, he'll perform better if he knows there's an informed client looking over his shoulder. And when it comes to picking that "right" accountant, look for one who is a deal maker as well as a well-schooled professional. Those with a little spirit in their blood are most apt to understand the kind of venture you are building.

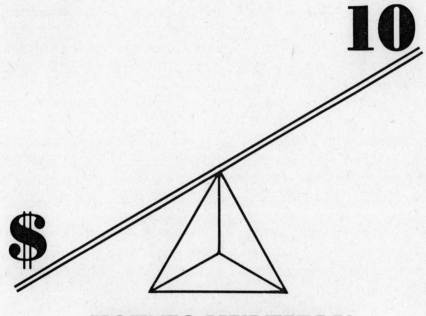

HOW TO MULTIPLY
THE POWER OF
THE CASH YOU RAISE

There is one key principle that we cannot repeat enough: leveraging means more than simply borrowing money or attracting investors. You must know how to make the most of cash once it comes flowing into your accounts. And believe it or not, that can be much harder than it seems.

A WHOLE NEW SET
OF RULES

The biggest problem is in overcoming the old cliches about the way a business should be run. Remember, this is not a traditional, run-of-the-mill, Main Street U.S.A. business, where things are done the way they have been done for centuries.

Nor is this to be managed the way you have always run businesses before (providing you are an established business owner seeking to expand your interests). This is a leveraged venture, and that implies a whole new set of rules and principles for the way the company should be run.

First, let's debunk the old notion that the business owner must be the chief cook and bottle washer at all of his firms. That the entrepreneur must personally do or oversee all functions regardless of how minor or mundane they may be. The owner who acts on this premise supports the notion that "if you want something done right, you must do it yourself." Actually, the person who truly believes this is a slave to it. By arrogantly insisting that he or she alone is capable of handling even minor details, the owner gets bogged down in a mess of time-consuming details that add little to profits and, quite contrary to the intended effect, really deprive the firm of its growth potential.

Why do we say this? Well, let's examine the deeper implications of wearing all the hats in any business. What this really means is that you are willing to serve as a part-time secretary, janitor, clerk, receptionist, mechanic, store manager and so on. You see yourself as a hired hand, as little more than a common laborer. Is that any way to get rich? Of course not.

The truth is that most individuals approaching leveraged entrepreneurship will have to thoroughly rethink their entire attitude about running a business. You must consider your time far too valuable to be spent on menial tasks. You must abandon the romantic, work ethic notion of being "married," so to speak, to a single store, plant or service company. The successful leveraged entrepreneur must, instead, devote the great bulk of his talents, energies and time to multiplying the power of the cash he has raised.

He must utilize the process of "capital seeding" to magnify the worth of his cash assets many times over.

Capital seeding refers to the concept of using the cash you have raised to start a number of business ventures. Think of it as a farmer with a bag of seed. He can either throw all of the seeds in one spot or spread them across many acres. The former approach will yield one plant and a good deal of wasted seed; the latter will likely produce a bumper crop and a bountiful harvest.

The same procedures can be applied to the building of business ventures. Entrepreneurs can invest all of their cash in one company and then devote their lives to that firm, adding more and more cash to the same enterprise. But, as leveraged entrepreneurs, we think there is a better way.

Like the farmer producing a bumper crop, why not spread your cash over a wide range of business interests. There's no reason why the same entrepreneur can not own and invest in restaurants, tennis courts, discos, apparel shops, casinos and laundromats—the sky is the limit. If you play your cards right and have some luck, each can yield a handsome return, taking you from the ranks of the comfortable to the very wealthy—from the business-owner category to that of tycoon or industrial magnate.

To get this far, however, you will have to abandon that old notion we've mentioned about doing all the jobs in your companies yourself. You will have to give up some of the management hats to others. When you are on your way to building an empire of business ventures, there's no way that you can get bogged down with minor details at any single firm. The trick is to start thinking of yourself as an expert in raising money and putting it to the most productive use. That's your specialty—and it's one very few among us can claim. You concentrate on this—on raising capital and seeding it—and let others do the day-to-day chores for you.

In saying this, however, we must make one thing clear from the start. We do not suggest that an owner start a business and then simply walk away from it to start another. That is neglect—the kind of poor management that frequently leads to business failure. What we suggest, instead, is striking a delicate balance between giving a venture too much or too little attention. Certainly, as the owner, you must retain overall responsibility for your companies. You must be fully briefed on their activities and you must call all of the really important shots. When it comes to long-range planning and other crucial management decisions, the buck will definitely have to stop at your desk. This much is clear.

But those chief cook and bottle washing jobs—and the function of daily management—can be assigned to others while you focus on the big picture. This very act of delegation is the first step in capital seeding because it frees the principal entrepreneur to pursue those really essential activities. There are, however, great dangers in the concept of delegation, and pitfalls to be accounted for in the system of delegation recommended to you. The greatest danger is that those entrusted to conduct various aspects of your business will be careless, indifferent or lax in their work, or worse yet, will, due to jealousy, seek to sabotage your firm. This can take various forms from absenteeism to mistreatment of customers to intentional damage of company property.

Dangers such as these are what cause many owner-managers to believe that they must be at the place of business to open in the morning and on hand to close up at night. That as soon as the cat is away, the mice will play. But it doesn't have to be this way at all. We contend that the leveraged entrepreneur can devote his time to expanding and developing his commercial interests while others faithfully and effectively run and manage his individual firms on a daily basis.

SETTING UP AN INCENTIVE PLAN

The secret to this "balancing act" is the incentive system. By making your employees—each and every one of them—partners in the firm's success, you will all but guarantee their dedication to the betterment of the business. Once there is something in it for them— once they have a share of the pie—most jealousies, antagonisms and laziness are redirected into ambition, drive and hard work. They will want the company to succeed and will therefore put in their best performance whether or not you are there to supervise. This, alas, is your ticket to entrepreneurial freedom. What's more, even if you have no intention of leaving your place of business for a single day, the incentive plan would aid your company immeasurably. Regardless of how tough a supervisor you are, people work better when they are motivated by a carrot before their noses rather than by a whip on their backs.

So, the incentive plan has a double-barrel benefit. It not only makes it possible for the entrepreneur to parcel his time and energies out to a number of ventures simultaneously, but it also tends to improve the financial performance at each individual outfit. Net profits can easily climb by 25 percent whenever effective incentive plans are instituted. Multiply that substantial increase by several companies and you can be talking about millions of dollars of extra profit. That is one of the ways to multiply the power of the cash you raise.

Exactly what kind of incentive plans do we have in mind? Well, we believe that to be effective, the plans have to extend beyond the traditional limits which give incentive bonuses only to top executives. To our way of thinking, every employee can add or detract from a firm—and so each and every one of them should have a stake in the venture. Incentive bonuses should be awarded to all employees, from the sweeper to the senior vice president.

For every year that the company increases its profitability by ten percent compared to the previous year, the following percentage bonuses should be tacked on to employees' salaries:

- Five percent for secretarial, clerical and other low-ranking workers.

- Seven percent for skilled workers including technicians, production experts and mechanics.

- Ten percent to semi-professional white collar employees below the management level and to production foremen or supervisors.

- Fifteen percent to middle management and professionals including accountants and researchers.

- A full 25 percent to top management and to those sales representatives whose efforts can have a major impact on the firm's revenues.

In addition to this overall program, a competition should be held for the Employee of the Year in each of the above categories, with the winner judged on the basis of their contribution to the firm's earnings. These select individuals should be granted bonuses of 50 percent of their annual salaries. The effect of this is to get all employees competing among one another to do the best possible work for the company. What more can an owner dream of?

To make the incentive plan have the utmost psychological effect, it should be clearly announced to all employees at meetings addressed by the owner and by a brief pamphlet describing the guidelines. It must be made clear that bonuses will be awarded only in those years that earnings increase by at least ten percent. Also, the winners of the Employees of the Year Awards should be given the checks at a company party so that their good example will be fully recognized by all others.

One noted practitioner of a fine incentive plan is the highly-successful Friendly Ice Cream Co. This once-family-operated outfit of small ice cream parlors, has grown to a chain of several hundred units and most experts agree that its success is due, to a great extent, to the fine quality of its store managers. Rather than taking the traditional route of treating managers as glorified clerks at the low end of the salary scale, Friendly puts its managers on bonuses that reflect the performance of the stores they run. For this reason, the manager of its Mt. Kisco, N.Y. store, for example, is known to make about $50,000 a year.

If you think that's too much for a manager of a small restaurant, hear this: the shop generates more than $1 million a year, is constantly improving its performance and is highly profitable. Friendly shops are extremely clean, service is prompt and all employees are polite and courteous. The owner of the firm doesn't have to be there, because the manager on the scene shares in the action and considers himself a partner in the company's success.

"I took the unusual step of putting my mechanics on a bonus plan," says Geoff A. of Wheeling, West Virginia, the owner of a chain of 22 tire and auto service stores. "And I did it for a good reason."

"I was out raising money to expand from a one-store operation to a chain, and every time I added an additional outlet, it seemed as if I had more and more troubles. The mechanics hired to staff the stores would goof off when I was gone, wouldn't show up for work when I needed them most and had the attitude that they would try to get away with as much as possible and still get a day's pay.

"So my organization and I were really working against one another. I was out trying to build up the business and the people who did the work were acting to tear it down. I would get mad as hell about this state of affairs until one day it dawned on me that the mechanics had no reason to care about the business as much as I did. I promised them the same salary if the business was humming along or gasping for breath. Why knock themselves out of it wouldn't make any impact on their take home pay?

"That's when I started our "Junior Partner Bonus Plan," basing each mechanic's extra compensation on the profitability of the shop he worked in. If the shop on Beekman Street boosted its profits while the unit on Third Avenue took a loss, only the mechanics at the Beekman outlet got incentives. That way, no group of employees could go along for a free ride on the sweat of others."

Geoff's plan exceeded even the most optimistic projections. Absenteeism was slashed from a 20-percent factor to less than 2 percent, profits increased an average of 18 percent per store and existing customers began to compliment Geoff on the quality of his staff. The sales increases prompted bankers to lend Geoff the funds required to launch additional units and he was able to secure more favorable interest rates to boot.

"The mechanics even started coming to me with money-making suggestions," Geoff adds. "Like getting licensed as state motor vehicle inspection stations. The fees for inspections were negligible, but we were able to pick up extra business related to compliance codes. Another man recommended that we start selling diesel fuel and offering diesel repairs in order to cater to the growing number of diesel vehicles on the road. Both ideas brought in an additional $3.1 million last year alone—and, of course, part of that went right to the staff. The men feel like they own part of the shops, so the operations hum whether I am on the scene or not."

Once the entrepreneur is free from the duties of daily management, he can concentrate on expanding his business or breaking into new types of ventures. This is what capital seeding is all about.

The question is, at what point can the owner feel safe enough to relax some of his first-hand control of the business? When can he feel free to leave the manager in charge and to devote more attention to other ventures? Certainly, no successful entrepreneur will open a firm, hang out his sign, hire employees and then leave things to run on their own right away. But when can the break be made? Although there are no hard and fast rules here, I suggest that the time for considering such action takes place once the new business—or the one seeking expansion—has passed the break-even point. It is at this point in time that the founder can have some assurance that the business is well on its way to stable growth, that all systems and procedures are ironed out and that his constant attention is not required on the scene. He can then move on to seed his capital in other ventures—expanding the width and breadth of his business empire.

To put it simply, the woman who obtains $200,000 in business start-up funds can put $100,000 into her first concern, a personnel agency. Once this reaches the break-even point, she can put another $25,000 into a convenience grocery, $25,000 into a home products distributorship and $25,000 into an ice cream store franchised unit. Each one of these units, once they pass the break even point, can then be used to attract even more expansion capital from banks or investors. Through this seeding process, the initial $200,000 can produce funds of up to ten times its value. Of course it is not easy—and the businesses must be well run—but it can be done.

Let's take a closer look at what we mean by this all-important break-even point. Break even volume is the sum of total fixed costs (costs which do not vary with the level of business activity) divided by the selling price minus the variable cost per unit of merchandise sold. It looks like this:

$$\text{Break-even volume} = \frac{\text{Total fixed costs}}{\text{Selling price} - \text{variable cost per unit}}$$

Using a hypothetical example, the ABC Corp. figures the costs for one of its products as follows: total fixed costs, $100,000; variable cost, $50 per unit. The selling price for the item is $100 per unit. This means that $50 per unit can be applied towards fixed costs. With fixed costs of $100,000, 2000 units will have to be sold before any profit is earned. From that point on—after fixed costs are recovered—the $50 per unit sold will be profit.

The break-even point of 2000 units is figured as such:

$$\frac{\$100,000}{\$100-\$50}$$

Break-even volume = 2000

Entrepreneurs can use a break-even chart to study the same data in more detailed and visible form. The real benefit of the chart is that the distance between the two sloping lines shows the amount of profit and/or loss that can be expected at the sales volume represented by that point (see chart).

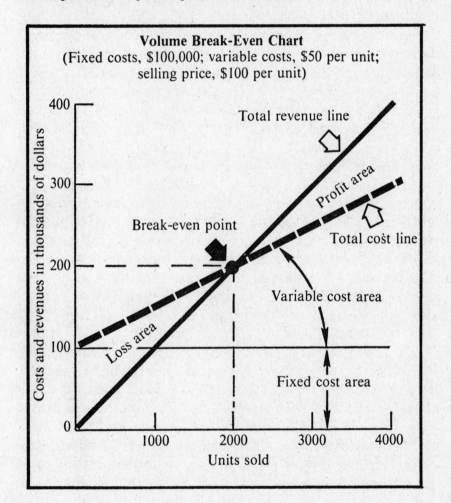

Volume Break-Even Chart
(Fixed costs, $100,000; variable costs, $50 per unit;
selling price, $100 per unit)

As a leveraged entrepreneur, you will want to use break-even charts to determine when it is appropriate to relax your day-to-day controls of a business venture—when you are free to turn over daily responsibilities to incentive plan managers.

"Simply because a company reaches or passes the break-even point does not mean its future is assured or that it is on the way to robust profitability," says Martin L., a tax attorney and accountant based in Cambridge, Mass. "But it can be taken as a signal that the firm, especially in a startup situation, has overcome its most difficult hurdles and will survive and make it over the long run. I have found that the intensive supervision by the principal owner is no longer as necessary once the break-even point is passed and is sustained for a significant period of time."

Two of Martin's most important clients are leveraged entrepreneurs who have used the break-even point indicator as the key element in their business-building strategies. Paul K., a skilled plumber, and for years an independent tradesman, who answered daily calls for his skills from home builders, home owners and contractors, recognized from the number of gripes he heard that people were fed up with high plumbing bills. Realizing that something could be done to tap this consumer unrest (every seeming problem is actually an opportunity in disguise), Paul thought of opening a small shop that would sell plumbing supplies and instruction kits to do-it-yourselfers.

"Like most people who come up with a brainstorm, I treasured the idea in the back of my mind but never acted on it," Paul notes. "That is, until I told the missus about it. She thought it was a great idea, and since she has more guts than me when it comes to investing money, she demanded that we take our $37,000 savings from the Bankers Trust and start the shop."

The rest, as they say, is history. The Mr. Plumber store enabled the average homeowner to cut plumbing bills by up to 55 percent. Once the press picked up on this and started doing anti-inflation features on the business, the shop was booming. Five more stores were added in the second year of operations.

"I watched everything like a hawk in those early years," Paul notes, "and I'm glad I did. We had to set up procedures that would guarantee good customer service, the proper inventories and an orderly flow of business. Just deciding what parts we should stock in great quantity, which we should keep small inventories of and which should only be specially ordered took a good year of experience."

DEVELOPING PROBLEMS AND SOLUTIONS

With this behind him, however, Paul was eager to open more and more shops. Mr. Plumber was a proven money-maker and the banks were willing partners, extending expansion capital and a healthy line of credit. By the fourth year, Paul had a greatly-expanded operation with 22 stores in three states, a staff of 450 employees and annual revenues of $9 million. But he also had problems. Some of the newer stores were not grossing nearly as much as the older units. Alarmed by this trend, Paul's wife (again, the real business brains behind the operation) hired Martin L., to look into the developing problems and to recommend solutions.

After closely examining the business for more than a month, Martin identified the cause of the troubles. As a leveraged entrepreneur, Paul was successful in raising money and in building his branch network mostly on borrowed funds. The problem was, however, that success went to his head—he became so preoccupied with expansion that he ignored the nuts-and-bolts requirements of good management. Paul was leaving his newer stores to swim on their own too soon—before the necessary systems and procedures were worked out and store managers could take over the reins.

"What Paul didn't realize," Martin explains, "is that the systems he set up for his early stores did not always apply to the newer ones. That's because the later units were built in different areas, serving different types of people, with different income levels and different types of homes. Stocking faucets for turn-of-the-century tubs made sense in one location, but were an absolute joke in another where there was little but contemporary homes.

"That's when we hit on the break-even point strategy. We came to see that once the units achieved break-even status, the kinks were already worked out and Paul's presence on a daily basis was not required. We used this approach to put the troubled stores back on sound footing and to expand the business to a total of 51 units.''

What's more, Paul's great success with Mr. Plumber made him a much sought-after partner for all sorts of business deals with moneyed investors. Literally millions of dollars of cold cash was offered to him, much of it from European and Oriental investors seeking to participate in the U.S. economy. With the advice of his wife and his attorney, Paul graduated to the big leagues, seeding this investment capital into car dealerships, an amusement park, a meat packing house and a country club. All of his deals were made on a silent partner basis (that's the way he wanted it) and all were nursed along to the break-even point, when Paul then moved on.

At this time, Paul sits in a huge, elaborately-furnished office in New York's World Trade Center. The head of a mini-conglomerate, he now owns and oversees 16 companies producing annual revenues of $43 million a year. Paul, the former plumber, wears $550 custom suits, is chauffer-driven to and from his Tudor home in Scarsdale N.Y. and vacations for three full months a year. He is the first to claim that he owes it all to a rational, systematic and intelligent approach to leveraged finance.

*   *   *   *   *   *

What we are noting here is that to multiply the power of the cash you raise—and that is an integral part of successful leveraging—you must establish ventures that produce the max-imum level of profits. This has a snowball effect in that it vastly increases the bottom-line return to you and, through this greater earnings performance, enables you to tap the best loan and invest-ment sources. I therefore suggest that you take a blank notebook and make headings and notes for the following ways to cut business costs and boost profits.

You must learn to "do things the right way"—to be an agile and responsive manager, constantly exploring and welcoming ways to keep down the high cost of doing business and to push up the amounts and the margins of profits you draw.

Look beyond what the textbooks and the business professors say. Stop concentrating all your time and effort on a single area of expertise. Start looking at the broad sweep of your business and audit every single activity to make sure you are getting the "best bang for your buck". Do this and you will be on your way to the kind of heads-up management required for today's tough and competitive markets.

To help you get started check the following list of little-known ways to build business profits. Try to incorporate these ideas into your company's operations and search for the many hundreds of other obscure services just waiting to slash your costs and swell your earnings. Remember, there are two ways to build profits: slash costs and boost sales.

1. Sales Agents

Roughly 50 percent of the nation's small business failures are directly attributable to insufficient sales. This operating deficiency is serious and widespread, affecting firms in a broad cross section of industries.

The problem of inadequate volume can generally be traced to the sales department staff: poorly trained, misguided or unmotivated. In some cases, the department itself may simply be too small or lack effective management. In any case, salesmen are not producing sufficiently to keep the company operating profitably.

Rather than start a lengthy and uncertain process of revitalizing the sales staff, management may opt to engage an outside sales agent. This alternative offers a quick solution to the problem at hand and may prove to be an ideal way for the firm to operate on a permanent basis.

Agents are paid only for results and are therefore never a drain on revenues. Because they work independently, selling for numerous clients, the agents are not on the small company's payroll. They do not draw a salary, benefits or travel expenses. The only charge for their services is the specified commission, significant only if they are generating substantial volume.

It's a good idea for the company owner-manager to compare the salaried and agent marketing systems. The following criteria may help management make the right choice in this vital decision: Unless a relatively small number of salesmen produce a tremendous volume, it is usually less expensive to hire agents than full-time, salary-plus-commission representatives. In addition, using agents enables the firm to obtain representation in marginal territories where new business levels are not sufficient to support a staff salesman. If the situation changes and the market demonstrates rapid growth, a full-time man can be employed.

The names of suitable agents may be obtained from executives in non-competing firms and from trade magazine salesmen and editors. In addition, agent listings are available from the Manufacturer's Agents National Association, Alhambra, Calif., and from the National Council of Salesman's Organizations, New York City.

2. Bad Debt Insurance

Credit losses cost the nation's businesses more than $3 billion annually and the toll is rising. High bankruptcy rates and poor payment practices are forcing more and more companies to write off bad debts at substantial losses.

Managers can, however, reduce the likelihood of substantial losses by tightening up credit standards and by buying bad-debt insurance. This little-known type of insurance coverage offers financial protection against sudden losses due to customer bankruptcies.

Bad debt insurance (technically known as commercial credit insurance) is a specialized service available through a handful of concerns known as credit insurers. Some carriers are units of major insurance companies; others are small independents specializing in this service. Although the terms of their policies may differ somewhat, most carriers offer the same general types of coverage.

Commercial credit coverage is a form of "excess loss insurance". It is a guarantee to manufacturers, jobbers, wholesalers and service companies that they will be reimbursed for bad debts sustained in excess of a specified deductible.

Coverage fees vary according to the amounts of money involved and the level of risk to the insurer. Policyholders with a history of poor collection practices will pay more than those exercising tight credit controls. In general, fees for bad-debt insurance amount to roughly one percent of the sales volume covered.

In return for this fee, policyholders may submit slow-paying accounts to the insurers as soon as payments are deemed delinquent. The insurers then have 60 days from receipt of the claims to meet with the policyholders for the purpose of settling the accounts.

The insurer then acts as a collection service, working with the accounts to achieve payment in full. Policyholders pay no fee for this service if full collection is achieved within 10 days of the initial claim. Fees are charged to the policyholder if collection efforts continue beyond the grace period.

Policyholders may collect up to their coverage limits on all accounts which become insolvent or which remain uncollected after the 60-day period. All legal forms of insolvency are recognized and no service fee is charged for collecting the covered portion of insolvent accounts.

3. Resource Exchange

One of the best business bargains around is also one of the newest—natural resource exchange services. "We believe our service represents an idea whose time has come," says the president of the Natural Resource Recycling Exchange. "We make it possible for small and mid-size companies to purchase industrial materials, by-products and finished merchandise at substantial savings. At the same time, we help others dispose of waste materials in full compliance with environmental laws."

Here's how the service works: From time to time, most large corporations produce materials they cannot sell. Much of this is waste material—scrap metals, lubricants and chemicals from industrial processes—others are component parts and finished products left over from excess production.

A good deal of this "excess" and "waste" may be useful to small companies seeking cheap sources for business products and materials. Resource exchanges help to supply this need by finding buyers for traditionally unsalable materials.

Small companies benefit by obtaining any number of things—from electrical parts to calculators—at prices between 20 and 40 percent cheaper than through traditional outlets.

The Natural Resource Recycling Exchange does most of its matchmaking between buyers and sellers by way of a specially programmed computer. Information on available materials is coded and fed into the system; the same is done for data on potential buyers. When a match is made, the exchange notifies both parties and helps to negotiate the deal.

The exchange's fees vary according to the services rendered. A simple listing in the computer system costs $250 annually. For this price, the small company may list as many items as it wishes to buy or sell.

Companies interested in this service may contact any of the following: Natural Resource Recycling Exchange, 286 Congress St., Boston, Mass. 02210. American Chemical Exchange, 4849 Gold Rd., Skokie, Illinois 60076. Iowa Industrial Waste Information Exchange, Iowa State University, Ames, Iowa 50011.

4. Interconnect Communications

One of the best opportunities to save big on business costs is in the area of communications—the telephone to be precise. Thanks to some welcome Federal Communications Commission rulings, it is now possible for small companies to switch from leasing Bell system equipment to buying their own.

The savings potential is enormous—and for this reason thousands of firms are taking the plunge: giving up Ma Bell's costly rental rates and switching to telephone ownership instead. The move means not having to pay Bell's monthly equipment fees for the life of the firm; the ability to get specialized types of equipment and the substantial tax advantages available to companies that buy rather than lease phone equipment.

The hundreds of companies that have rushed to serve this new market are known as "interconnect" outfits—they sell the equipment that is "connected" to Bell's lines.

The opportunities for saving are substantial. Take this example drawn by an interconnect executive: "a hypothetical company with a key telephone system using 20 phones and 12 trunk lines could save about $235 per month for equipment for the first five years of use. Then, after the purchase payout period, the saving would be about $600 per month. What's more, management would get an immediate tax credit in the year of purchase."

Enough said. Check the yellow pages under Communications Equipment for the names of interconnect suppliers. Be sure to get several competitive bids before acting.

5. Computerized Credit Bank

Even one delinquent account can spell serious trouble for small company budgets. Cash flow deteriorates, for example, and that means the creditor's own buying power is reduced. Management cannot replenish inventories, purchase supplies or cover overhead. The impact of the problem is clear: Up to 26 percent of industrial bankruptcies are attributed to bad debts.

A computer service can help to reduce this toll. Sponsored by the National Association of Credit Management, the service helps small companies protect themselves from poor credit risks. Managers can now obtain fast, accurate and economical credit checks on prospective customers before shipping a dollar's worth of merchandise.

Here's how the service works: Five hundred participating businesses provide the National Credit Information Service with detailed statistics on their customers' payment records. The data is transmitted on magnetic tapes and is entered into the NACIS central computer. It is then available for use by NACIS subscribers.

The firms providing information cover a wide cross-section of business and industry. Many are large corporations with thousands of customers of their own. For this reason the system can provide detailed credit information on up to 2 million companies.

NACIS credit reports include the following information:

• **The amount of money the company owes each reporting supplier.**
• **A breakdown of each amount owed, as to how much is current, how much is 30 days old, 60 days old, 90 days old or older.**

Certainly, this is only a partial list of profit boosting techniques that should go hand-in-hand with your leveraged cash-raising strategies. Remember, one reinforces the other. Keep an eye out in the business press and in trade association newsletters for other novel ways to cut your costs and bolster the bottom line.

You now have all of the essentials required for launching, managing and expanding a leveraged business enterprise. In the next chapter, I will concentrate on the ways to accumulate the most personal wealth from these business earnings.

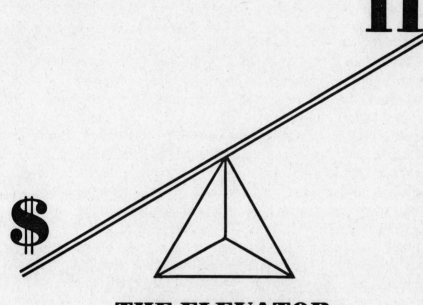

THE ELEVATOR
PRINCIPLE:
HOW TO MAXIMIZE
YOUR PERSONAL WEALTH

One of the real tragedies of business life is that many individuals who achieve significant success in the commercial world never manage to translate this success into personal wealth. It happens far too frequently: The noted industrialist or merchant grants a press interview and claims to have little in the way of liquid assets—everything is tied up in the business. The public, which is not at all familiar with the intricacies of high finance, refuses to believe the man's claims, saying "the nerve of him to plead poverty. He should know what it's like to be really poor."

The public's attitude is understandable, to be sure. Compared to the average laborer or even to the corporate executive, our successful entrepreneur is, in fact, very well off. His cry is not one of poverty but of lost potential. The individual who has built a major business enterprise should not be compared to the average worker—he has a right to expect more in terms of personal wealth, a great deal more. And when these expectations are not reached, there is good cause for disappointment; for a bit of self-pity.

Sadly enough, this wide disparity between an entrepreneur's corporate wealth and his personal assets is a common state of affairs. A life of hard work and dedication to a business yields a lifestyle which is often comfortable but not extravagant—the trappings of true wealth are never attained. This leads to frustration during the individual's active career, a diminished standard of living in retirement and an estate that does not provide amply enough for the heirs (or which forces them to sell the business simply to pay the taxes).

I say that some self-pity is quite understandable in these cases. The person who has used his talents, energies and intelligence to establish a successful business venture is entitled to some regrets when the fruits of this labor do not pour over into the personal column. True financial security and enjoyment of the high life—with its villas, yachts and butlers—can come only when the individual builds up a margin of wealth that is private—separate from the corporate structure. This is especially true in terms of today's tax laws, which make it very difficult to allocate business funds for personal luxuries. So, as we say, some disappointment at not having personal wealth is only natural.

THE SECRET OF ACCUMULATING WEALTH

But—and this is the crucial point—you must recognize that the failure to accumulate personal wealth is, for successful entrepreneurs, not a matter of the fates. It is a matter of poor planning aided by a lack of information. The entrepreneur has no one to blame but himself. Any one with the drive, the ambition and the savvy to establish a major business organization could and should have significant personal wealth to match. The failure to have this half of the success equation is not the fault of society, bureaucrats, the tax system or the dilution of free enterprise. Although there are drawbacks to our economic system, it is still very possible to translate the assets of your leveraged business enterprise into substantial personal wealth. Many business owners do it, and I'll show you how.

Just how this is accomplished is based on what we call the "elevator principle"—this means using the income, bonuses, dividends and other payments earned from business operations to build a foundation for personal wealth and then utilizing little-known techniques to parlay that wealth into ever-greater sums. This is termed the "elevator principle" because it enables the entrepreneur to rise above the standard socioeconomic classes and to join the top ranks of society—the privileged few.

Elevator techniques are based partly on the principles of leveraging that were used in the development of your corporate organization and also on concepts of tax sheltering, sound financial advice, thorough planning and the discovery of obscure but very valuable financial devices. It is most important to bear in mind, at all times, that outstanding business success should not be viewed as the end-all objective; using your leveraged power to build personal wealth is the goal. That means you'll have to devote some time to the personal as well as to the corporate side of your life. As you are actively engaged in "capital seeding" many ventures, keep one eye on the home front as well. Although it is acceptable to have financial consultants—including accountants and tax attorneys—to help you with this, never delegate complete control to others. You and you alone will have to pay the price if there is no cash in the bank at the end.

Leveraging plays only a part in the elevator principle, because cash borrowing techniques are less critical here than in the corporate phase of your ventures. When it comes to the personal side, we take a more prudent approach: most of the cash income required to build personal wealth comes from the highly-leveraged business side. There is little need to raise money here but instead to parlay, accumulate and protect it. So caution and sound, insider techniques are the name of the game.

LEVERAGING PERSONAL ASSETS

Leveraging of personal assets comes into play mostly as a stock market strategy. Although I do not suggest investing heavily in blue chip stocks (there are other equally safe approaches that can yield much more), your personal game plan should include some action in speculative growth issues. Here, I suggest isolating emerging public companies in the industry you are most familiar with and investing in those firms which your experience tells you will expand rapidly. No more than two speculative issues should be played at any one time, and in no case should they attract more than five percent of your personal investment capital.

The key point is to use your insider information to pick growth stocks. Why rely on questionable market newsletters or know-nothing stock brokers when you can use your knowledge of a particular industry to select the most promising ventures. Jack R., owner of a leveraged mini-empire that included 26 dry cleaning stores poured $36,000 into the shares of another, larger dry cleaning outfit that went public.

"I knew they were a first rate operation—something the general public had no real way of telling," Jack explains. "So I bought 18,000 shares at the offering price of $2 each. Within a year I sold out and earned a tidy profit of $46,000 after commissions. I always invest in the industries that I know from personal experience—that gives me a leg up on the average person."

The leveraging in stock market transactions comes in the use of margin accounts. Although this is a relatively simple and easy-to-use strategy, far too many investors fail to take advantage of it. Margin accounts simply let you control larger volumes of stock with less cash up front. All you are required to do is to put up a percentage of the purchase price to buy the number of shares that you want.

Let's say that you purchase stock on a 50-percent margin basis. To buy 10,000 shares of Stock A at $10 a share (total value of $100,000), you would need only send the broker $50,000—but you would still control all 10,000 shares. So if the stock went up $5 per share, you would still net the full $50,000 profit (minus commissions). Of course, declines in the per share price will trigger margin calls, requiring you to fork up more money to the broker to retain your control of the stock.

Buying on margin is an important part of the elevator principle, because it enables you to get the most bang for your buck in this part of your investing strategy. I believe in tying up as little cash as possible in the market (better to place your money in unique or limited edition classic items such as art, antique automobiles, stamps, coins and tapestries) and margin buying helps us to do this without diminishing our control of selected growth issues.

Keeping track of your margin transactions—and separating business from personal finances—is easier now then ever before. That's because the age of computerized personal finance is here. With all the wizardry of sci-fi robots, automated money managers now handle everything from balancing checkbooks to checking family budgets. This service is one of those little-known business devices that are integral to the elevator principle—to giving you that edge you need to accumulate the highest amount of personal assets.

For the self-employed, the application of computer power to personal finance is right on target. Most leveraged entrepreneurs have unusually complex finances: yours is a mixed bag of personal and commercial transactions that can be too much for even the experienced layman to handle. The sheer volume of the paperwork alone deprives you of more productive management time.

USING COMPUTER ANALYSIS

"Many small business people err by never clearly delineating between the two financial worlds: business and personal," says Frank Proietti, president of PDS Computer Corp of Englewood, N.J. "By meshing the two together—and by keeping poor records for both—they often lose out on investment dividends, tax deductions and business opportunities. We take the tedium of financial management so that they can make more profitable decisions."

Computer outfits like PDS can help straighten out financial affairs by performing comprehensive analyses of business and personal transactions. Although this service has been available to big corporations for years, it is just now becoming widely available to smaller users.

Working from remote computer processing centers, these outfits take raw data from their clients, code the data and then report back monthly or quarterly with a clear picture of the client's finances. The objective is to provide individuals with current and comprehensive information on their investment portfolios, tax deductions, dividend and interest income and business performance.

"Most self-employed people have stock market holdings," says Lawrence Simon of Wall Street Concepts, Inc., New York. "But since they are usually preoccupied with running their own companies, they rarely have the time to properly supervise their stock portfolios. There simply aren't enough hours in the day to do it all.

"That's where we come in. We have the client's broker send us confirmation slips of all transactions and security positions. We monitor these holdings and prepare comprehensive reports detailing the value of current holdings, gains and losses for tax purposes, performance of the portfolio compared to the Dow Jones and Standard & Poor averages and a comparative check on the broker's performance."

Other major analyses offered by the computer outfits include:

1. Personal Checkbook: A running record of all personal expenses is compiled on a monthly basis. Expenses are categorized by type of tax deduction, such as medical, charitable and interest payments. Clients provide the raw data by forwarding non-negotiable duplicate copies of all checks.

2. Balance Sheet: Designed to keep owner-managers up-to-date on their companies' operating performance, balance sheet analyses include income statements, comparison to budgets, comparison to previous year's performance, cash flow projections and liquidity ratios.

3. Time and Billing Administration for Professionals: Figuring monthly client billing reports can be a tedious job for busy professionals like lawyers, accountants and engineers.

Even a small law firm, for example, can have several thousand billable transactions a month. Each incidence of client contact must be recorded, assigned an hourly rate, multiplied by the rate and totaled. Computer services assume the full burden of this time-consuming function.

It is important to keep in mind that most computer financial outfits serve as statisticians, not advisors. Their strengths are limited to analyses of completed transactions. Most offer their services nationally.

Clients do appear pleased with the service. "PDS is handling both my business and personal records," says New York entrepreneur and investor Alfred R. "I have rather complex dealings and they put it all together so that I can exercise effective supervision."

It is important to note that the computer services do monitor both sides of the coin: personal as well as business finances. Your company's balance sheet as well as your personal stock portfolio can be reviewed by the computer. This is vital because there is a direct correlation between the amount of income that you have for personal use and the efficient and profitable operation of your company. Generally speaking, the more your business earns, the more you can shift over to the personal column. So although I have been stressing in this chapter the need to give a good deal of time and attention to personal finances—and although I have claimed that a successful business does not assure personal wealth—I do not mean to intimate that one is more important than the other. They are closely interrelated.

One of the ways to get more business income flowing through for personal use is to utilize every legal technique available to slash corporate income taxes. Here again, we have a little-known device to help you accomplish this: it is a prudent tax shelter or "tax haven."

THE MATTER OF TAX SHELTERS

The national craze over tax shelters has led countless investors to explore the alleged wonders of cattle feeding, oil drilling and equipment leasing. All of this frantic activity is directed towards a single objective: to put more money in personal accounts and less in Uncle Sam's.

Preoccupation with the more exotic schemes has, however, obscured the fact that some of the best tax shelters are safe, straightforward and easy to use. Investing in so-called "tax havens" is a good example. Here, profits from commercial operations are subject to little or no taxation—and it is all perfectly legal and aboveboard. For U.S. small business owners, the best of the tax havens is Puerto Rico.

Puerto Rico is a self-governing commonwealth in union with the U.S. The dollar is the official form of currency and local residents are American citizens. The main attraction of the island from a business standpoint is that U.S.-based businesses operating subsidiaries there save roughly $700 million per year in federal taxes.

The tax savings—made possible by unique government policy—are specifically-designed to lure businesses to the island. Puerto Rico's large and growing labor pool requires constant infusions of new business to satisfy the demand for jobs. By granting tax exemptions to U.S. companies, the government encourages investors to open plants and offices there.

"We are really rolling out the welcome mat for small companies," says Manuel Dubon, administrator of Fomento, the island's economic development agency. "The tax advantages available here make it possible to expand a new venture rapidly because most of the profits can be plowed back into the company."

Most important for small business, the island's new tax law exempts the first $100,000 of eligible corporate profits from all taxation. For earnings above that level, the amount of exemption varies with each of the commonwealth's four geographic regions. Greater tax breaks are available to U.S. companies locating subsidiaries in the underdeveloped regions outside the commercial centers of Ponce and San Juan.

Under current laws, mainland companies opening qualified ventures in Puerto Rico are entitled to a 90-percent tax exemption for the first five years, 75 percent for the next five and then a gradual leveling off to a 50-percent exemption after 20 years. The number of years of tax exemption granted to a firm again depends on the geographic region in which it locates.

U.S. business owners investing in Puerto Rico can bring profits from island operations back to the mainland at any time. These funds are subject to a small "tollgate tax," payable to Puerto Rico, but are free from taxation by the U.S. government. Entrepreneurs can avoid payment of the tollgate tax by reinvesting profits in Puerto Rican ventures.

"We opened a plant in Puerto Rico three years ago and it has proven to be a major success," says Fran G., vice president of a plant headquartered in Lindenhurst, NY, a maker of communications devices. "We have reinvested our profits there, expanded the size of our plant and tripled the number of employees."

"There is no comparable tax situation in the world for U.S. corporations," says a spokesman for the U.S. Treasury Dept. "Not only do the Puerto Rican subsidiaries enjoy substantial tax exemptions on their local operations but repatriated funds are also free from U.S. taxation. This is a unique situation: Profits repatriated from other tax-exempt areas are usually subject to U.S. taxes."

Leveraged entrepreneurs interested in exploring tax-exempt business ventures in Puerto Rico can make contact with the commonwealth's Economic Development Administration, 1290 Avenue of the Americas, New York City, N.Y. (212-245-1200).

Business investments in Puerto Rico are recommended for those firms putting a high premium on financial incentives. And, as a leveraged entrepreneur, that includes you. The power of your business earnings for building personal wealth can be many times greater when they are not diluted by stiff federal income taxes. This is precisely why the "tax haven" strategy is so congruous with the elevator principle: The overall objective here is to gain the maximum levels of raw business income that you can then accumulate for substantial personal wealth.

ANOTHER IMPORTANT SECRET

What other devices are available to you that can translate business success into personal luxuries? How else can you use the power and fortune of a successful commercial enterprise to bring material comforts? What else does your standing in the business community give you that can have impact on the acquisition of cars, boats, jewelry and the like?

Before answering these questions, I would like to share a pearl of wisdom once given to us by a wealthy furrier. When asked his secret for accumulating an enormous fortune valued at more than $20 million, he said, "Always remember, it's not only how much you make that counts, but also how much you save."

What he meant here is that many entrepreneurs become so preoccupied with making money, that they overlook the possibilities for saving money—for acquiring the things they want, need or have always dreamed of having at lower than usual costs. This, too, adds to your personal wealth, and it brings us to another of those little-known services on which the elevator principle is built. (Keep in mind that you are out to do everything possible to reach the highest standards of living.)

The money-saving strategy referred to by the furrier boils down to the old familiar come-on "Wanna buy it wholesale?" It's part of a service that can save you up to 50 percent on the purchase of products and services.

The service is based on the oldest known form of business trade: bartering. A number of national outfits have updated this ancient practice, added computer controls and made it a bargain bonanza for many small companies.

Here's how it works: business owners and professionals simply trade their own goods and services for the goods and services of others. An accountant in the market for business equipment, for example, agrees to prepare tax returns in exchange for a minicomputer; a clothing manufacturer trades coats for stereo equipment.

"We act as a central clearinghouse for this trading," says Jean Louis Janssen, vice president of Business Exchange, Inc., a nationwide bartering outfit. "Ours is much like a banking function: we match buyers and sellers, provide members with monthly printouts of their barter transactions and compute the balance in their accounts.

"We also issue the major negotiating tools, called BX checks. Members fill out these checks—the same way they use regular bank checks—to buy goods and services from one another. Venders send the checks to us and we then credit their accounts for the sale and debit the accounts of the purchasers."

Here's where the cost savings come in: a clothing retailer can barter a $400 suit in exchange for $400 worth of tennis equipment. Since the suit actually cost the retailer only about $200, the merchant is actually purchasing $400 worth of tennis equipment for $200. The same formula applies regardless of the merchandise involved: members can use goods purchased at or near wholesale costs to obtain other goods at full retail value.

"It's almost like buying dollars with 50-cent pieces," Janssen boasts. "Once a member sells a product or service, we credit his account for the full retail price of the sale. This credit can then be used towards the purchase of any other items in the barter inventory."

Lists of products and services available to members are published regularly by the barter exchange. In addition, trade specialists employed by the exchange can be called on to track down hard-to-find merchandise and to arrange special deals. The major barter agencies can handle everything from small trades of consumer goods to major transactions involving commercial buildings, machinery and real estate.

"The Business Exchange has just about doubled my purchasing power," says jeweler Morris W. "I've been a member for three years and in that time I've bartered jewelry items for vacations, clothing and gifts. The service is a real find."

Unlike centralized barter outfits which arrange both ends of all transactions, personalized services like the Business Exchange leave the buying and selling to members. The head office simply services special requests, processes transactions and keeps the records.

Membership fees for the Business Exchange are $159 for initiation, $36 annual dues and a monthly service charge of eight percent of gross purchases.

Applications and additional information are available from two leading barter outfits: Business Exchange, 4716 Vineland Ave., North Hollywood, Ca. 91602 and Mutual Credit Buying Service, 9200 Sunset Blvd., Los Angeles, Ca. 90069. Or, check the white pages of local directories.

The real beauty here is that the entrepreneur is once again using the power of his business standing to net personal gains. Just like the dry cleaning president, who invests in publicly-owned dry cleaning outfits, uses his business connection as a stock market weapon, you can use your business connection for raw purchasing power.

*   *   *   *   *   *

To sum it all up, the elevator principle means, first and foremost, drawing on your strengths in the commercial or corporate sector to achieve personal wealth. It makes all the sense in the world. Why fight it out on the same level and on the same terms with the millions of dreamers, schemers and opportunity seekers who do not have the clout of a successful business organization behind them? Why invest in the same stocks everyone else is buying when you have valuable insider information on the industries in which you are actively engaged? Certainly, acting from your positions of strength makes much more sense. You have an advantage: use it. I would also like to repeat my admonition that you stay away from the stock market (except for one or two speculative investments). As mentioned previously, the pure investment part of the elevator principle calls for limiting most investments to real estate, art, classic automobiles and the like.

We say this for good reason: no other investment vehicles offer equal opportunities for capital appreciation with minimum downside risk. Take Woody R., a Ft. Lauderdale entrepreneur who invested $37,000 six years ago in two colorful and dynamic works of art by Calder. The treasures have beautified his home immeasurably, have been the objects of envy and admiration by friends and business associates and have quadrupled in value in this relatively short time.

"The great thing is that unlike the stock market or other types of traditional investments," Woody adds, "there's virtually no chance that these works will ever lose value. They'll just get more and more valuable all the time. I won't have to go through the heartache my stock market investor friends have of waking up one morning to find that the Dow Jones averages have fallen by 30 points and they've lost $100,000 in one day."

No one type of art or limited edition investing is intrinsically better than the others. Classic automobiles, paintings, coins, stamps, rare books, even autographs—all have great potential. The key point is to do careful research into the field you choose before investing a dime.

The best approach is to make the investment activities a source of pleasure and relaxation rather than work. Take it on as a leisure time activity. This will take the burden out of investing and will give you the double satisfaction of knowing that your off-work hours are also profitable. Visit museums, read art books, talk with curators and collectors, attend auctions, subscribe to specialized magazines. The more you know, the better informed your decisions will be and the greater your edge over other investors.

Although this combination of leisure and investment activities is the ideal situation, I do recognize that for some busy entrepreneurs, the two parts of their lives must be totally separate. For many, once there is profit involved, there is no opportunity for real relaxation. To these individuals, and to all investors who would like some objective review of their strategies, I recommend making contact with a professional investment adviser. This can be for a continuing relationship or a limited number of consultations. You must be aware, however, that the field of investment advising is flooded with the good and the bad, the qualified and the quacks, the ethical and the rip-off artists. Trying to find a competent practitioner to help with your personal financial strategies can be difficult.

The task can be made easier by obtaining a copy of the Directory of Investment Advisers Registered with the Securities and Exchange Commission. The directory lists, by state, all of the 400 investment advisers registered with the SEC. The publication is especially useful in that it tells how to obtain the SEC file on any registered investment adviser. The file includes names, educational and business background and the professional experience of the advisers. The publication is available from Source Securities, 70 Pine St., N.Y., N.Y. 10005.

* * * * * *

There you have it: the complete guide to harnessing the power of leveraged finance, from the pure business end to the personal side. Now the ball is in your court. The rest is up to you.

Good luck

Index